Rhyming Wranglers

Cowboy Poets of the Canadian West

Rhyming Wranglers

Cowboy Poets of the Canadian West

Selected by Ken Mitchell

Frontenac House
Calgary, Alberta

Book and cover design: Epix Design
Cover photo: Ted Grant
Author photo: Don Hall

Library and Archives Canada Cataloguing in Publication
    Rhyming wranglers : cowboy poets of the Canadian West / Ken
Mitchell, editor.
Poems.
ISBN 978-1-897181-13-3
    1. Cowboys--Poetry. 2. Cowgirls--Poetry. 3. Ranch life--Poetry. 4.
Canada,
Western--Poetry. 5. Cowboys' writings, Canadian (English). 6. Canadian
poetry
(English)--Canada, Western. I. Mitchell, Ken, 1940-
PS8279.R49 2007   C811.008'0921636213
 C2007-900863-1

We acknowledge the support of the Canada Council for the Arts for our publishing program. We also acknowledge the support of The Alberta Foundation for the Arts.

**Canada Council
for the Arts** **Conseil des Arts
du Canada**

Printed and bound in Canada
Published by Frontenac House Ltd.
1138 Frontenac Avenue S.W.
Calgary, Alberta, T2T 1B6, Canada
Tel: 403-245-2491 Fax: 403-245-2380
editor@frontenachouse.com   www.frontenachouse.com

For Kyra

Contents

Rhyming Wranglers

Cowboy Poets of the Canadian West

FOREWORD

There is a cultural movement sweeping the Western plains like a prairie fire: cowboy poetry. In gatherings and festivals from Fort Qu'Appelle to Pincher Creek, from Maple Creek to Stony Plain (and beyond), these cowboy poets are chanting the praises of the ranching culture as never before – in numbers unimagined in the days before the automobile and the airplane spelt the end of horsepower. Cowboy poetry has become a popular phenomenon in both Western Canada and the United States.

Cowboy poetry is a folk art – perhaps more performance art than literary – and it began its long history among the cattle herders, farmers and settlers of the North American frontier about 1870. It evolved from campfire songs and tales, often appearing in newspapers and self-published booklets, and circulated through oral recitation. The genre favours narrative poems in the ballad form, popularized by poets like Rabbie Burns, Rudyard Kipling, and Robert Service. Such poetry became rooted in the widespread cowboy culture that evolved in the 20th century, mythologized through Western movies, rodeos, stampedes, and other media.

There is, however, a modern turning point in its development. The new era of cowboy poetry can be dated by a single event: the first Cowboy Poetry Gathering in Elko, Nevada in January of 1985. The American National Endowment for the Arts funded a group of artists to organize a conference on cowboy poetry, music, and storytelling. Led by Hal Cannon, director of the Western Folklife Center in Elko, the organizers sought out the sources and resources of this oral tradition, and sent out a call for practising poets and story-tellers. One of those artists was Canadian folk singer Ian Tyson, who in recent years has also taken up horse ranching in Alberta, to occupy himself when he is not performing and recording his cowboy songs.

The success of the Elko gathering was astonishing. Hundreds of cowboys (and cowgirls), story-tellers, poets, musicians, and folklorists came together in a celebration that was part revival meeting and part craft fair. Elko instantly became a mecca for cowboy poets and Western historians, and the Annual Cowboy Poetry Gathering has been held every year since, with ever-growing crowds attending. "The Gathering" is now the raison d'etre of this town of 18,000 people, an oasis of poetry in a vast desert landscape, 200 miles west of Salt Lake. Elko is to cowboy poetry what Nashville is to country music.

Moreover, cowboy poetry festivals and gatherings have sprung up in hundreds of locations throughout Canada and the U.S. It has the raw excitement of a cultural movement, as performers travel in circuits throughout the West, writing and performing ballads in halls and cattle arenas from El Paso to Whitehorse. The "gatherings" are often held in conjunction with horse sales, rodeos, or livestock exhibitions, such as the Calgary Stampede and Regina's Canadian Western Agribition. The events attract audiences in the thousands – far more than attend the average literary reading.

Most modern poets and literary critics do not see, or hear, cowboy poetry as "real" poetry, probably because it still hews to traditional rhyme and regular meter, which can sound quaint and old-fashioned to academic ears. There is little free verse performed at a gathering, though there are notable exceptions, such as the work of Sid Marty and Thelma Poirier, or the American Paul Zarzyski. It seems that the cowboy poem's appeal among working people in rural communities lies in its song-like metrical form. Indeed, it is closely related to the cowboy songs which evolved out of the same tradition. In performance it is rarely read from a page, but is usually recited from memory, often accompanied by music. Like rap and hip-hip poetry, it is a counter-cultural phenomenon, and defiant in its resistance to the mainstream of literary poetry.

There are any number of themes in cowboy poetry, but they tend to cluster around (a) ranch life, (b) animals, usually horses or cattle, (c) the raw beauty of nature, (d) rodeo action. Many are comic or satirical, relying on situational humour and regional dialect to generate their effect.

Possibly the best working definition of cowboy poetry was written down and approved at the 1985 Elko Gathering by Mike Korn, a Montana folklorist:

Cowboy Poetry is rhymed, metered verse written by someone who has lived a significant portion of his or her life in Western North America cattle culture. The verse reflects an intimate knowledge of that way of life, and the community from which it maintains itself in tradition. Cowboy poetry may or may not in fact be anonymous in authorship but must have qualities, content and style which permit it to be accepted into the repertoire of the cultural community as reflecting that community's aesthetics in style, form and content.

The structural style of cowboy poetry has its antecedents in the ballad style of England and the Appalachian South. It is similar to popular works of authors such as Robert W. Service and Rudyard Kipling.

To be authentic, a poem should have most of these characteristics, and be delivered in Western gear – a Stetson hat and cowboy boots are essential wear at cowboy poetry gatherings. Above all, though, the poem should be expressed in the vernacular of the West, the spoken language of common wranglers, stockmen and cowgirls.

There have been several anthologies of American cowboy poetry published in recent years, and an interesting volume by Red Deer Press, *Riding the Range*, a definitive cross-border anthology. There is also *Bards in the Saddle*, a 1997 publication of members of the Alberta Cowboy Poetry Association. For this "all-Canadian edition", I have selected the best historical and contemporary Canadian cowboy poetry I could find. The Glenbow Museum archives in Calgary offered up a small treasure of historical nuggets – long-forgotten pamphlets and crudely published chapbooks that have customarily defined the poet's need to be immortalized in print. I also attended gatherings in Canada and the U.S. to listen and learn the craft at first-hand. Naturally there is a lot of bad cowboy poetry out there – verse riddled with clumsy syntax, worn-out cliches, and shrill sentimentality. Much of it is forgettable doggerel. But there's bad poetry everywhere, and the best cowboy poems – as I hope to demonstrate here – achieve literary status for their witty and colourful language, their social insights, and their moving stories.

This is, of course, a somewhat eclectic edition, including such major (but outlaw) poets as Sheri-D Wilson, Sid Marty and Corb Lund. But you will find they all speak the authentic lingo of the cowboy. I hope you enjoy this treasury of Canadian classics of the campfire. A final word of advice: to become infused with the Spirit of the West, it is best to read these poems aloud. Remember, it's the sound that informs.

ANONYMOUS

*The oldest cowboy song I could find in Canada was the lyrics to "The Opeongo Line", an Ottawa Valley folk song dating well back to the 19th century. It was first collected by the Rev. Joseph E. Gravelle of Otter Lake, Quebec and published in Edith Fowke's collection **Lumbering Songs from the North Wood** (NC Press, 1985). Thanks to poet Phil Hall for sending it along.*

The Opeongo Line

On the Opeongo Line
I drove a span of bays
One summer once upon a time
For Hoolihan and Hayes.
Now that the bays are dead and gone
And grim old age is mine,
A phantom team and teamster start
From Renfrew, rain or shine –

Ay, dreaming, dreaming, I go teaming
On the Opeongo Line.

ARTHUR PEAKE

There are many versions of "The Strawberry Roan" but the best Canadian one was written by Arthur Peake, who emigrated from England to the Northwest in 1884. Peake took up ranching in the foothills country south of Calgary before moving to open range country along the Red Deer River in 1897, the setting for his poem "Home". There he raised horses and cattle near the town of Dorothy, until he died in 1947. A book of his poems, Ballads From the Badlands, was published by Coyote Books in 1991.

The Strawberry Roan

Come all you old buckaroos and listen to my rhyme
About the ol' bronc rider that didn't have a dime.
How he tried to ride a pony, and tried to ride him fair,
And found himself a-sitting on nothing in the air.
For I would like to tell you this rider of renown
Was born and bred a cowboy and did not live in town.
He was raised down in Texas and rode the Chisholm Trail
And all his life had followed up the old cow trail.

About the old roan pony this feller couldn't ride;
Well no one ever rode him, tho' several of them tried.
He went wild up in the mountains and the cowboys called him Chief;
So they named a mountain after him, and that is my belief.
All around the campfires they talked of the Strawberry Roan
Who never joined a bunch again but always ranged alone.
They say he fought a puma once and chased him to his lair,
And it wouldn't have surprised me if he'd killed a grizzly bear.

The Indians in the lodges too, still speak of him by name;
For after trailing him for days they could not win the game.
Many wild horse hunters who thought he'd come up short
Just saw a flash of the strawberry roan and heard his fearful snort.
He made for the big tall timber and travelled far and wide;
He wintered with the deer and moose and knew just where to hide.

Home

It's years ago since first I crossed Red Deer
And roughlocked down those broken banks of clay,
And built my home of cottonwood and willow
And hauled supplies from Gleichen far away.
The antelope then bunched upon the prairie,
And prairie chicks in thousands we did see,
And with haystacks in our yard when it came winter
The old Red Deer just looked like home to me.

Our cattle ranged from Willow Creek to Bullpound;
The open range was good and free to all.
We branded calves, cut hay and then the beef herd
Was gathered up for shipping in the fall.
A rider then he headed for the rancho
Says "A welcome there and feed for horse and me."
We talked on brands, bits and spurs and saddles,
And the old Red Deer just felt like home to me.

Now it's lonesome today beside the old Red Deer;
The riders they no longer come this way.
The range is fenced and cut up into homesteads,
For years we have not even talked of hay.
Beside the Red Deer's banks I have to linger,
Tho' the future here does not shine bright for me.
Could he hit the trail again for open country?
For freedom and feed, how happy we would be.

CHARLIE MILLAR

Another pioneering poet was the Illinois horse wrangler Charlie Millar, who migrated to the Northwest Territories in the 1880s. He and his brother worked at the legendary Bar U Ranch for the North West Cattle Company. Millar published his poem "On the Sale of the Bar U" in the Calgary Eye-Opener in 1902, shortly after George Lane took over the ranch. The Bar U is now a national heritage site.

On the Sale of the Bar U

The shades of night were falling fast
And the Bar U ranch was reached at last
For the YT boss had a telegram
That knocked from the roost the great I Am
Who said, "Goddimit!"

The great I Am did cry and moan
So he lifted his foot and kicked a stone
And dear little somebody made an awful fuss
When she left the ranch with the poor old cuss
Who always said "Goddimit!"

It lifted a load from the cowboys' heart
When they saw the old fellow ready to start,
For he docked their wages on a stormy day,
And the way they kicked you would hear him say
"Goddimit!"

The Nitches will miss their bread and jam,
Since they lost their friend the great I Am,
For he's gone to the East perhaps to stay,
And no more the cowboys will hear him say
"Goddimit!"

The great I Am is now no more
And old George Lane will take the floor,
He'll tell the cowboys what to do,
And shake them up with a
"Goddamyou!"

KATE SIMPSON HAYES

*Pioneer feminist Kate Simpson was born in Dalhousie, New Brunswick and left her husband behind to move to Regina, North West Territories, in 1885. There she fell in love with Nicholas Davin, the fiery Irish-Canadian politician and founder of the Regina Leader. Under the pseudonym Mary Markwell, Kate published one of the first books of verse in the west, **Prairie Pot Pourri**, in 1895. "Lower-Flat Annals" appeared in **Derby Day in the Yukon** (Musson Book Company, Toronto, 1910) under the pseudonym "Yukon Bill".*

Lower-Flat Annals

When we lived in Lower-Flat us folks know'd where we was at;
But them Eastern folks come, puttin' on great style:
Us Old-Timers, we all said we was better we was dead,
F'r th' way they talked an' acted, raised our bile.

They interduced new dances – thing-a-me-bobs called – "Lances"—
Where they traipsed up an' down upon th' floor,
A-bowin' and a'scrapin' (lords an' ladies they was apin'),
Th' Red River Jig? 'Twa'n't never danced no more!

Sniffed at bannock – sniffed at bacon; then, dried apples, they was taken;
An' that good old dish "plum-duff" went out th' door;
Then "part singin'" in th' church – "A choir" up in a perch –
And a "Tenner" from th' city. Say, y'should a-heard HIM roar!

Then the pretty little crea'cher, boardin' 'round, th' country Teacher;
(Her we fought about f'r dances in th' barn)
SHE went out o' date; a "perfesser" come t' prate
About ologies an' colleges; things childern COULDN'T larn.

Then they started "makin' calls," ketched Pa in his over-alls;
But he met 'em with a "How'dy!" at th' door;
The place was in a clutter – Ma, she was churnin' butter,
An' Pa fetch'd 'em in th' kitchen, an' they didn't "call" no more.

That was Mrs. Mumble-Mumps. Say, she DID put on humps;
Took her daughter Gwendolina t' furrin lan's,
An' they say paid out shin-plasters t' the one o' them Old Masters
F'r t' make a bust of Gwendolina's hands!

Gone was th' good old days, and gone th' good old ways
When an invitation meant th' fambly all;
When th' little an' th' big would crowd into th' rig,
An' th' fiddle livened up th' Chris'mus Ball.

It was "Welkim, welkim, Boys!" Lots of laughin', lots of noise;
With the babies piled like cordwood on th' floor;
Boys an' girls all dancin' – old folks too got prancin' –
An' th' supper? Say, we'd eat ontil we couldn't hold no more.

But them Eastern folks fetched "Style"; changed all that in a while;
Printed tickets told th' folks they was "to-home";
Served the supper frum "a buffey," an' they acted kind o' huffy
When our children round the parler used t' roam.

House was full of bricky-brack; china tea-pot with a crack –
An' they sort o' boasted of it; set it out t' common view;
Talked about the'r "Fambly Tree" – good land! Why, they know'd that we
Had ninety acres of 'em – scrub-oak bluff – an' poplars too!

Then Miss Mary Ellen Jones (her that come from Pile-o'-Bones)
Lived in nothin' but a mud-shack all her life,
She got puttin' on some airs, an' her nose jes' said, "Who cares?"
And th' District Member picked HER f'r a wife.

She did cut a silly caper: had her envelopes an' paper
Painted with a little brand in blue sot up on top;
When th' Flat laugh'd, I'll be blest! She said, "It's Poppa's crest!"
Well! Providence, that year, hailed out their crop.

But Mary Ellen's fall come when they gave th' weddin'-ball;
Invited all th' stylish folks – gave us th' glassy eye;
But says Pa, "Th' next election we'll bust th' damn connection,
F'r th' District Member goes out on th' fly!"

He he'er'd that. He wanted votes. So them stylish printed notes
Come trailin' in t' us who'd been rejected;
But Mary Ellen said (underlined in ink bright red),
"PLEASE UNDERSTAND NO CHILDREN IS EXPECTED"!

That joke went far an' wide, us folks laugh'd ontil we cried;
But Retribution it was on th' Distric Member's shins,
F'r that sassy little bride who behaved so very snide,
Inside a year perduced a pair of TWINS!

Since that time we get on better. Mary Ellen wrote a letter
T' th' weekly paper, statin' "District Member liked our ways";
Yes, Lower Flat's grow'd quite a place, runnin' other towns a race;
But ther' ain't th' fun we had them good old days!

WALTER FAREWELL

*Farewell was as close to Anonymous as a poet could possibly be. None of his work was published in his lifetime (1879?-1955). He was a reclusive drifter who moved west from Ontario and homesteaded near Edam, Saskatchewan, where he took up the profession of bootlegging. Folklorist Michael Taft came across three tattered scribblers of his poems and wrote a biography of Farewell, **The Bard of Edam** (Turner-Warwick Press, 1992), which includes several of the pioneer's primitive verses. My favourite is "Song Above the Dead", included here with misspellings intact. Taft dates it to around 1902.*

Song Above the Dead

Let us drink to the corpse that is laid in its box,
For his generous bump was a big as an ox;
Let us hope that in heaven with whisky he's crammed –
If he can't beat them all I'll concent to be damned,

How oft we've been drunk by the weight of his purse
Till our bodies reeled wide and our brains they were worse!
Then fill high the horns till our reason it rocks,
To old Hankie the boozer, stretched out in his box!

Close, close was he joined to the rod and the gun,
And the sport of the spear in the jack-lighted dun:
Oh, how sure where the salmon flashed down through the rocks,
Shot the steel of Old Hankie, now stiff in his box!

The far duck sits calm on the tide of her lake,
Tho' a hundred guns strive her existance to take;
But her blood dyes waves when his weapon unlocks –
The unerring old Marksman, now laid in his box

The old mud-cat thinks he's superior to man,
For he's tasted the fish worms of many a can;
But he nibbles once more, and the cunning old fox
Is landed by Hankie, so cold in his box.

Soon the pathway he's trodden we also must tred –
Through the dark gates of death to the land of the dead,
Where we shall, if our hopes don't get smashed on the rocks,
Live again with old Hankie – no more in his box.

ROBERT W. SERVICE

*Though often called "the Canadian Kipling" and "the Poet of the Yukon", the nationality of Robert Service remains uncertain. Born in England to Scottish parents, he emigrated to Canada in 1894. "The Cremation of Sam McGee" appeared in his first book, **Songs of a Sourdough**, published when he was a bank teller in Whitehorse, Yukon in 1907. It became one of the most widely recited poems of the twentieth century, and is still popular at cowboy poetry gatherings across the continent. After the success of his early books, Service moved to France, where he died in 1958. "The Quitter", though less known, may be a better poem.*

The Quitter

When you're lost in the Wild, and you're scared as a child,
And Death looks you bang in the eye,
And you're sore as a boil, it's according to Hoyle
To cock your revolver and …die.
But the Code of a Man says: "Fight all you can,"
And self-dissolution is barred.
In hunger and woe, oh, it's easy to blow…
It's the hell served for breakfast that's hard.

"You're sick of the game!" Well, now, that's a shame.
You're young and you're brave and you're bright.
"You've had a raw deal!" I know – but don't squeal,
Buck up, do your damnedest, and fight.
It's the plugging away that will win you the day,
So don't be a piker, old pard!
Just draw on your grit; it's so easy to quit:
It's the keeping-your-chin-up that's hard.

It's easy to cry that you're beaten—and die;
It's easy to crawfish and crawl;
But to fight and to fight when hope's out of sight—
Why that's the best game of them all!
And though you come out of each gruelling bout
All broken and beaten and scarred,
Just have one more try – it's easy to die,
It's the keeping-on-living that's hard.

The Cremation of Sam McGee

There are strange things done in the midnight sun
By the men who moil for gold;
The arctic trails have their secret tales
That would make your blood run cold;
The Northern Lights have seen queer sights,
But the queerest they ever did see
Was the night on the marge of Lake Lebarge
I cremated Sam McGee.

Now Sam McGee was from Tennessee, where the cotton blooms and blows.
Why he left his home in the South to roam 'round the Pole, God only knows.
He was always cold, but the land of gold seemed to hold him like a spell;
Though he'd often say in his homely way that he'd "sooner live in hell."

On a Christmas Day we were mushing our way over the Dawson trail.
Talk of your cold! Through the parka's fold it stabbed like a driven nail.
If our eyes we'd close, then the lashes froze till sometimes we couldn't see;
It wasn't much fun, but the only one to whimper was Sam McGee.

And that very night, as we lay packed tight in our robes beneath the snow,
And the dogs were fed, and the stars o'erhead were dancing heel and toe,
He turned to me, and "Cap," says he, "I'll cash in this trip, I guess;
And if I do, I'm asking that you won't refuse my last request."

Well, it seemed so low that I couldn't say no; then he says with a sort of moan:
"It's the cursed cold, and it's got right hold till I'm chilled clean through to the bone.
Yet 'tain't being dead – it's my awful dread of the icy grave that pains;
So I want you to swear that, foul or fair, you'll cremate my last remains."

A pal's last need is thing to heed, so I swore I would not fail;
And we started on at the streak of dawn; but God! he looked ghastly pale.
He crouched on the sleigh, and he raved all day of his home in Tennessee;
And before nightfall a corpse was all that was left of Sam McGee.

There wasn't a breath in that land of death, and I hurried, horror-driven,
With a corpse half hid that I couldn't get rid, because of a promise given;
It was lashed to the sleigh, and it seemed to say: "You may tax your brawn and brains,
But you promised true, and it's up to you to cremate those last remains."

Now a promise made is a dept unpaid, and the trail has its own stern code.
In the days to come, though my lips were dumb, in my heart how I cursed that load.
In the long, long night, by the lone firelight, while the huskies, round in a ring,
Howled out their woes to the homeless snows – O God! how I loathed the thing.

Till I came to the marge of Lake Lebarge, and a derelict there lay;
It was jammed in the ice, but I saw in a trice it was called the "Alice May".
And I looked at it, and I thought a bit, and I looked at my frozen chum;
Then "Here" said I, with a sudden cry, "is my cre-ma-tor-eum."

Some planks I tore from the cabin floor, and I lit the boiler fire;
Some coal I found that was lying around, and I heaped the fuel higher;
The flames just soared, and the furnace roared – such a blaze you seldom see;
And I burrowed a hole in the growing coal, and I stuffed in Sam McGee.

Then I made a hike, for I didn't like to hear him sizzle so;
And the heavens scowled, and the huskies howled, and the wind began to blow.
It was icy cold, but the hot sweat rolled down my cheeks, and I don't know why;
And the greasy smoke in an inky cloak went streaking down the sky.

I do not know how long in the snow I wrestled with grisly fear;
But the stars came out and they danced about ere again I ventured near;
I was sick with dread, but I bravely said: "I'll just take a peep inside.
I guess he's cooked, and it's time I looked"; then the door I opened wide.

And there sat Sam, looking cool and calm, in the heart of the furnace roar;
And he wore a smile you could see a mile, and he said: "Please close that door.
It's fine in here, but I greatly fear you'll let in the cold and storm –
Since I left Plumtree, down in Tennessee, it's the first time I've been warm."

There are strange things done in the midnight sun
By the men who moil for gold;
The Arctic trails have their secret tales
That would make your blood run cold;
The Northern Lights have seen queer sights,
But the queerest they ever did see
Was that night on the marge of Lake Lebarge
I cremated Sam McGee.

RHODA SIVELL

*Ms. Sivell was a pioneer ranching wife and poet at the turn of the century. I found her self-published volume of verses, **Voices from the Range** (1912), in the Glenbow Museum archives. There are a number of good poems in her collection, but "Come with Me to the Old Range" is one of the best evocations of the foothills ranching country that has ever been written. It is almost certainly the oldest.*

Come with Me to the Old Range

Come with me to the old range
Just for an hour or so;
You'll hear the call of the range stock
And the voice of the Chinook blow.
Blowing down o'er the wind-swept hills
Where the pups of the grey wolf play
And their dens lie deep in the hidden steep
Of the cut-banks far away.

You'll hear the song of the bluebird
As she swings on the willow tree,
And the note of the wild dove cooing;
See the range that looks good to me;
Hear the wild young range horse neighing,
The music of unshod feet,
And the sun o'er the range hills setting –
The things that make life complete.

You will smell the wild clematis,
As it falls in a cloud of white,
Sending its glorious fragrance
Far out in the prairie night;
See the moon shining over the river,
Hear the call of the coyote shrill,
And the long, deep bay of the lone wolf
Coming down from the far-off hill.

You will see Dick the bronco buster,
The rider who doesn't blow;
You will hear of the old, hard winter,
The crust on the frozen snow;
Of the outlaw hunted by redcoats
When he hid in the old range hills;
Of the mist that hangs over the river;
Of the soft rain that never chills.

Then come with me to the old range
Just for an hour or so;
I'll show the sweetest things on earth
Out where the Chinooks blow.

ALANSON BUCK

Little is known about Alanson L. Buck, beyond the fact that he served in the Canadian Army in the First World War and that his volume of poetry, **The Outlaw and Other Poems,** *was published by William Briggs Publishing, Toronto, in 1913. "The Stampede" is a characteristic saga from the later frontier days.*

The Stampede

The steers are wild and nervous,
    In that uneasy fear;
They moo and paw and bellow
    As though some wraith were near;
They move in restless circles,
    As the eve sinks black and drear.

They dread the dark'ning skyline,
    The hurtling shots of hail,
Those steel-ringed heralds,
    In magic voice of Baal,
That cut the grassy meadows
    To its under-clot of shale.
They fear the glaring glamour,
    Piercing from heaven's blaze;
They shirk the blast splendor,
    They reel before its maze;
They tremble in the lullings
    To the distress of craze.

Faster the lightning flashes,
    Thunder booms overhead;
They surge with insane folly,
    Then break in frenzied dread;
They're off with startles impact
    By common impulse led.
The spreading horns are tossing
    Like a storm-troubled ship;
They crowd to their undoing
    Where but the strong may grip;

What clamor and disaster
   Follows this headlong trip!

They shake the turf and batter
   The short, nutritious grass;
They trample out and shatter
   All that they meet; alas!
No obstacle can stay them –
   That dumbly crushing mass.

They're off with startled impact,
   And after drives the rain;
And many a purple nostril
   Blows out in throttled pain;
When the whole herd is plunging,
   Grim chaos in its train!

'Tis well no broken coulees
   Across the meadows drive,
Or else of all that frothing herd
   But few may long survive;
When hills and waters check them,
   Scarce one comes out alive.
Never the madness slackens,
   Till many a weary pace
Has passed and dropped in darkness,
   In this terrific race;
It seems unchecked to gather
   More fright in stubborn chase.

Heavens! what cruel torments
   Spring harshly from their eyes!
What painful devastation
   From where the stampede lies!
The greedy coyotes follow,
   With hungry yelps and cries.

They know a feast awaits them
    All trampled out, and spread;
They thus may gorge unhindered
    Till e'en the weak are fed;
They long may howl and scuffle
    Above the wanton dead.
'Tis then the cowboy tightens
    The saddle-girth; he spurs
Beside the steaming long-horns;
    With voice that thrills and stirs
The heaving brutes, he chides them,
    To check their wild demurs.

'Tis then the cowboy's mettle,
    If now he may be near,
Serves him so well and steady
    To rouse the herd with cheer;
So long that he has tagged them,
    He hates to lose a steer.
He edges up, condoles them,
    Shouts, sings some old-time chant,
He shoots in space to warn them,
    As the flanks still heave and pant;
He guides the circling fliers,
    So toil-worn, smoking, gaunt.

Slowly the hardy plainsmen,
    Without the least reproof,
Seek slow the home corral gate,
    The low and slanting roof.
They've saved the jaded cattle,
    The meek, the passive hoof.

ROBERT STEAD

Born in Ontario, Robert Stead moved to a Manitoba homestead with his family in 1882, at the age of two. He established and sold two weekly newspapers before he took up writing fiction and poetry set on the Canadian plains; his best-known work was a novel about farm life called **Grain** *(1926). "The Squad of One" was published in his first book of poems,* **Kitchener and Other Poems** *(Musson, 1917), although this version of the poem appeared in a later edition. "A Prairie Heroine" appeared in the same volume.*

The Squad of One

Sergeant Blue of the Mounted Police was a so-so kind of guy
He swore a bit, and he lied a bit, and he boozed a bit on the sly;
But he held the post at Snake Creek Bend in the good old British way,
And a grateful country paid him about sixty cents a day.

Now the life of the North-West Mounted Police breeds an all-round kind of man;
A man who can finish whatever he starts, and no matter how it began;
A man who can wrestle a drunken bum, or break up a range stampede –
Such are the men of the Mounted Police, and such are the men they breed.

The snow lay deep at the Snake Creek post and deep to east and west,
And the sergeant had made his ten-league beat and settled down to rest
In his two-by-four that they called a "post", where the flag flew overhead,
And he took a look at this monthly mail, and this is the note he read:

"To Sergeant Blue, of the Mounted Police, at the post at Snake Creek Bend,
From U.S. Marshal of County Blank, greetings to you, my friend:
They's a team of toughs give us the slip, though they shot up a couple of blokes,
And we reckon they's hid in Snake Creek Gulch, and posin' as farmer folks."

"Of all the toughs I ever saw I reckon these the worst,
So shoot to kill if you shoot at all, and be sure you do it first,
And send out your strongest squad of men and round them up if you can,
For dead or alive we want them here. Yours truly, Jack McMann."

And Sergeant Blue sat back and smiled, and his heart was glad and free,
And he said, "If I round these beggars up it's another stripe for me;
And promotion don't come easy to one of us Mountie chaps,
So I'll scout around tomorrow and I'll bring them in – perhaps."

Next morning Sergeant Blue, arrayed in farmer smock and jeans,
In a jumper sleigh he had made himself set out for the evergreens
That grow on the bank of Snake Creek Gulch by a homestead shack he knew,
And a smoke curled up from the chimney-pipe to welcome Sergeant Blue.

"Aha!" said Blue, "and who are you? Behold, the chimney smokes,
But the boy that owns this homestead shack is up at Okotoks;
And he wasn't expecting callers, for he left his key with me,
So I'll just drop in for an interview and we'll see what we shall see!"

So he drove his horse to the shanty door and hollered a loud "Good day,"
And a couple of men with fighting-irons came out beside the sleigh;
And the Sergeant said, "I'm a stranger here and I've driven a weary mile,
If you don't object I'll just sit down by the stove in the shack a while."

Then the Sergeant sat and smoked and talked of the home he had left down East,
And the cold and the snow, and the price of the land, and the life of the man and beast,
But all of a sudden he broke off with, "Neighbours, take a nip?
There's a horn of the best you'll find out there in my jumper, in the grip."

So one of the two went out for it, and as soon as he closed the door
The Sergeant tickled the other one's ribs with the nose of his forty-four;
"Now, fellow," he said, "you're a man of sense, and you know when you're on the rocks
And a noise as loud as a mouse from you and they'll take you home in a box."

And he fastened the bracelets to his wrists, and his legs with a halter-shank,
And he took his knife and he took his gun and he made him safe as the bank,
And then he mustered Number Two in an Indian file parade,
And he gave some brief directions – and Number Two obeyed.

And when he coupled them each to each and set them down on the bed,
"It's a frosty day and we'd better eat before we go," he said.
So he fried some pork and he warmed some beans, and he set out the best he saw,
And he noted the price for the man of the house, according to British law.

That night in the post sat Sergeant Blue, with paper and pen in hand,
And this is the word he wrote and signed and mailed to a foreign land:
"To U.S. Marshal of County Blank, greetings I give to you;
My squad has just brought in your men, and the squad was Sergeant Blue."

There are things unguessed, there are tales untold, in the life of the great lone land,
But here is a fact that the prairie-bred alone may understand,
That a thousand miles in the fastnesses the fear of the law obtains,
And the pioneers of justice were the "Riders of the Plains".

A Prairie Heroine

They were running out the try-lines, they were staking out the grade;
Through the hills they had to measure, through the sloughs they had to wade;
They were piercing unknown regions, they were crossing nameless streams,
With the prairie for a pillow and the sky above their dreams,
They were mapping unborn cities in the age-long pregnant clay,
When they came upon a little mound across the right-of-way.

There were violets growing on it, and a buttercup or two,
That whispered of affection ever old and ever new,
And a little ring of whitewashed stones, bright in the summer sun,
But of marble slab or granite pile or pillar there was none;
And across the sleeping prairie lay a little, low-built shack,
With a garden patch before it and a wheat-field at its back.

"Well, boys, we'd better see him, and he hadn't ought to kick,
For we'll give him time to move it if he does it pretty quick."
But scarcely had the foreman spoke when straight across the farm
They saw the settler coming with a rifle on his arm;
Some would ha' hiked for cover but they had no place to run,
But most of them decided they would stay and see the fun.

The farmer was the first to speak: "I hate to interfere,
And mighty glad I am to see the railway comin' near,
But before you drive your pickets across this piece of land
You ought to hear the story, or you will not understand:
It's the story of a girl who was as true as she was brave,
And all that now remains of her is in that little grave.

"I didn't want to bring her when I hit the trail out West,
I knew I shouldn't do it, and I did my level best
To coax her not to come out for a year or two, at least,
But to stay and take it easy with her friends down in the East;

But while I coaxed and argued I was feelin' mighty glum,
And right down in my heart I kep' a-hopin' she would come.

"Well, by rail and boat and saddle we got out here at last,
A-livin' in the future, and forgettin' of the past;
We built ourselves a little home, and in our work and care
It seemed to me she always took what was the lion's share;
God knows just what she suffered, but she hid it with a smile,
And made out that she thought I was the only thing worth while.

"She stood it through the summer and the warm, brown days of fall,
And of all the voices calling her she would not hear the call;
But when the winter settled its cold, white pall of snow
She seemed to whiten with it, but she thought I didn't know;
She tried to keep her spirits up and laugh my fears away,
But I saw her growing thin and ever weaker day by day.

"At last I couldn't stand it any longer, so I said,
'I think you'd better try and spend a day or two in bed
While I go for a doctor. It's only sixty miles.'
She gave a little wistful look, half hidden in her smiles,
And said, 'Perhaps you'd better, though I think I'll be all right
When the spring comes…' Well, I started out that night.

"I made the trip on horseback, and we floundered on all night,
And reached our destination in the early morning light.
But the doctor had gone out of town, – just where, no one could say,
And a lump rose in my chest that fairly took my breath away.
But I daren't stay there thinking, and my search for him was vain,
So I brought some wine and brandy and I started home again.

"Forgetful of my horse, I spent the whole night on the road,
Till early in the morning he collapsed beneath his load;
I saw the brute was done for, and although it made me cry,
I hacked into his jug'lar vein and left him there to die;
And then I shouldered the supplies and staggered on alone,
And thinking of my wife's distress, I quite forgot my own.

"She must ha' watched all night for me, for in the morning grey
She saw me stagger in the snow and fall beside the way,
And God knows how she did it – she was only skin and bone—

But she came out here and found me and dragged me home alone,
And she took the precious liquor that had cost us all so dear,
And poured it down this worthless hulk that's standin' blattin' here…

"I guess you know what happened: I lived, she passed away;
I robed her in her wedding-dress and laid her in the clay;
And every spring I plant the flowers that grow upon her grave,
For I hold the spot as sacred as the Arimathaean's cave;
And when the winter snows have come, and all is white and still,
I spread a blanket on the mound to keep out frost and chill.

"Folks say I've got a screw loose, that I've gone to acting queer,
But I sometimes hear her speaking, and I know she's always near;
And sometimes in the night I feel the pressure of her hand
And for a blessed hour I share with her the Promised Land—
Let man or devil undertake to desecrate my dead
And as sure as God's in heaven I will pump him full of lead."

They were rough-and-ready railway men who stood about the spot,
They were men that lied and gambled, they were men that drank and fought,
But some of them were sneezing, and some were coughing bad,
And some were blowing noses on anything they had;
And some of them were swallowing at lumps that shouldn't come,
And some were swearing softly, and some were simply dumb.

At last the foreman found his voice: "I guess your claim is sound;
I wouldn't care to run a track across that piece of ground…
We'll have to change our lay-out… but I hope… we have the grace
To build a fitting monument to mark that holy place;
Put me down for a hundred; now, boys, how much for you?"
And they answered in a chorus, "We'll see the business through."

The passengers upon a certain railway o'er the plain
See a shining shaft of marble from the windows of the train,
But they do not know the story of the girl-wife in the snow
And the broken-hearted farmer with his lonely load of woe,
And none of them have guessed that the deflection in the line
Is the railway-builders' tribute to a prairie heroine.

CATHARINE BOND DICK

*Born in 1891 in Nova Scotia, Catharine Bond moved west with her family at the turn of the century to the foothills of southern Alberta. She married J.W. Dick in 1914 and became a partner on her husband's cattle ranch. They retired to Calgary in 1935. He published her volume of verse, **Trails I've Ridden, Alberta Range Rhymes** in 1946 (Alberta Job Press, Calgary). "Yesterday" appeared in that collection, and exemplifies the cowgirl spirit of that bygone era.*

Yesterday

We rode the range at dawning,
We rode the range at noon,
We camped out in the starlight
Beneath the bright full moon.

We jingled in the horses,
When the frost was cold and still,
Each man caught up his "private"
Ere the sun peeked o'er the hill.

Those days are dim and haunting –
They'll never come again,
The purple range at twilight,
The dripping hills of rain.

The round-up and the range-life,
They've faded with the years,
But memory comes to mock me,
And my heart cries out with tears.

A.L. "SCOTTY" FREEBAIRN

Scotty Freebairn published several volumes of verse and stories in the 1950s, including **Rhymes of an Old Timer***, which featured his classic piece, "The Big Fight". Fairbairn had been born in Ayrshire, Scotland, around 1880, settling in Pincher Creek, Alberta with his parents in 1899. He became a community story-teller and bard, collecting tales of the trader Kootenai Brown and other heroes of the Canadian West. Scotty's grandson John Mitchell of Pincher Creek in 2006 republished* **Rhymes of an Old Timer.**

The Big Fight

The boys from off the roundup
Planned to trim the sports in town;
They made a pool of all their dough
And how they'd put it down.
Van Cleave would ride the Cochrane horse,
In town few knew his name;
LeGrandeur for the Walrond
Had a lot more local fame.

The sports in town would surely bet
LeGrandeur's horse to win;
The Cochrane boys would bet it all
On Van Cleave to come in.
So July the First they headed
For the town of Pincher Creek,
And the annual celebration
That would last about a week.

The farmers and the ranchers
Came from forty miles or more;
The Indians from Brocket
With their families by the score.
The local band played lustily,
Jones sold the betting pools;
The judges and the starters
To enforce the racing rules.

There were racehorses from Calgary,
From Lethbridge and the 'Hat;
Jockeys dressed in silks and satins,
Pancake saddles and all that.
There were races for the two-year-olds,
Five furlongs and the mile,
While the cowboys waiting patiently
Could scarce repress a smile.

At last the cowboys' saddle horse
Was lined up for the start,
And perhaps a dozen riders
Got away not far apart,
But going down the back stretch
There were two well out ahead:
Van Cleave and young Le Grandeur,
But, by jove, LeGrandeur led.

Around the turn they galloped,
Young LeGrandeur still ahead;
The cowboys with their money up
Were wishing he'd drop dead.
Would the kid in his excitement
Forget to let Van win;
And that's exactly what he did,
He batted it right in.

Old timers still recall the fight
That night in Dobbie's bar;
Some rider claimed it was a frame
Pulled by the W.R.
LeGrandeur took a poke at him
That laid him on the floor,
And soon it was a free for all
With six or seven more.

Bolster, Gunn and Slivers
Were quick to take a hand,
And you couldn't say the Cochrane men
Were lacking much in sand.
It was hell and bloody murder,
Till the Cochrane took it back,
And the Walrond put the drinks up
Though the town had all the jack.

STANLEY HARRISON

*Stanley Harrison (1885-1980) was an English-born horse-breeder and local character who settled near Fort Qu'Appelle, Northwest Territories in 1902. He published a number of his verses during his lifetime, mostly in the **Thoroughbred Record**, a horse-breeders' journal out of Lexington, Kentucky. "The Cowboy" appeared in Grant MacEwan's biography of Harrison, **The Rhyming Horseman of the Qu'Appelle**, in 1978.*

The Cowboy

My song is of the cowboy,
The rider of the range
Whose master is Adventure,
Whose light o' love is Change;
Lean-visaged, lank, laconic,
He grins in mild disdain
At demonstrated sentiment,
But hums a sad refrain.
The sun is in his humour,
The earth is his reserve;
Slow speech and bashful bearing
But cloak an iron nerve.

He ropes a bucking renegade
Bow-bent for bitter strife
And once within the saddle
A centaur springs to life;
O shades of mythic Pegasus
Full-flight in watching wonder –
There leaps and lurches from its bonds
A blasting bolt of thunder;
Red rage within its heart and brain
It hurls its wrath upon
This Greek that dares to challenge Greek –
This chapped Bellerophon!

By simple tone and token,
By the bronco's shocking spring
His camp-fire knows a cowhand
His saddle knows a king.
With grazing herd and solitude
Of arching starry sky
And "paint" horse underneath him
To answer heel and thigh,
He rides a world of liberty
By compass of his own,
With chaps for shield and armour
And saddle for a throne.

PAUL HIEBERT

*Paul Hiebert (1892-1987) was a humourist as well as a Professor of Chemistry at the University of Manitoba. In 1947 he published a fictional biography called **Sarah Binks**, "the Sweet Songstress of Saskatchewan", which became a Canadian cult classic and a favourite of Peter Gzowski. It won the Leacock Medal for Humour for 1947, and included this delightful poem of Sarah's. "The Hired Man on a Saturday Night" is more parody than purity in the cowboy tradition, but the comic effect of Sarah's hired man ensures its survival round the campfire.*

The Hired Man on a Saturday Night

A horse! A horse! Give me a horse,
To dash across the frozen north,
And wallow in the mire,
A noble barb with cloven hoof,
With brazen wings and blatant snoof,
And molten eyes of fire.

I'll carve a furlong through the snow,
And bring the bastard she-cat low,
And bind her to a tree,
That ding-bat dire, shall put her sire,
Out of the frying pan into the fire,
Where e'er she be.

With gathered rage of many an age,
I'll blot the boar from off the page,
And twist his face;
I'll smite the rooster in the snow,
And crafty Rover, dumb with woe,
Shall curse his race.

I'll tie a reef knot in the tail
Of Barney's bull – with tooth and nail
I'll fill his day with gloom;
The calf shall wail, the cow shall quail,
The horse shall totter and grow pale –
Give me room!

GLEN RAFUSE

*Glen Rafuse was a veteran Black Angus rancher in the Mountney Valley near Fort St. John, one of the most northerly spreads in Canada. In later years he retired to Bowden, Alberta to write and perform cowboy poetry. For 30 years he was in great demand until he died in October, 2006 at the age of 70. The poem "Horses and Men" is part of his published collection, **"Life of a Stockman: the Poetry of Starchild".***

Horses and Men

They were gathered round the fire one night
These gray-haired time-worn men,
Just sippin' their beer and their coffee too
And recallin' those days "way back when".

When the Gang Ranch ran for a hundred miles
And your summer camp was a packhorse load.
When fences were made of jack pine rails
And the Chilko Ranch was the end of the road!

When the saddle you rode was centre-fire rigged
And your horse wore the JHG brand
When raisin' good steers took two or three years
And hay was stacked by horses and men!

And the wood that fired the big iron stove
Where you fed was all split by hand,
And the creeks and canals that watered the fields
Were all built there by horses and men.

And each man in turn spoke of lessons he'd learned;
Some remembered the blisters and pride
Of ten-hour days on the haystack
And the creak of that old "beaver-slide"!

No, they'd never forget old Jimmy Rosette,
The craziest breed on that old JH crew.
He was beat-up and lamed by the broncs he had tamed
And even bears—cause he'd roped quite a few!

There were boys who drove teams in the summer
And in winter hauled feed to the cows
On racks made of wood. Yes, those times were good
And you can bet that it's all different now.

But around that campfire there wasn't one liar.
These were cowhands from times "way back when"
As they noted with pride all those famous "wild rides"
And all the work done by horses and men.

HARVEY MAWSON

Harvey Mawson is a retired cowboy who makes his home at Dundurn, Saskatchwan where his family has been ranching for five generations, since 1882. Harvey is the author of several books of poetry, notably **Brimstone and Bobwire,** *and a book of short fiction,* **Cowboy Up, Rodeo Stories.** *In 1988, he was a feature poet at the Elko Gathering. He wrote "Northwest Passage" as a tribute to the Dirt Hills rancher Bill Pryor.*

Northwest Passage

Life at its best is bound to be rough
Well-suited to men who are double damn tough.
In shortgrass country where the hardy ones stay,
The wind takes the rest and blows 'em away.

Down in the Big Muddy there's many a tale
of a bronc-ridin' man who went up the trail.
For that hard scrabble of land there in the breaks,
Big Bill was a hand who had what it takes.

Tall in the saddle, a hard man to throw;
If there was horses in hell he'd be ready to go.
While ridin' full blast down a vertical slope
He'd choke down the devil with a sixty-foot rope.

In a Moose Jaw oasis Bill heard the talk
Near Dawson Crick they needed some stock:
Horses for saddle, wagon and pack,
History to write in a dusty hoof-track.

On a line-back buckskin he gathered his herd,
Set a course for the north like a migratin' bird,
Across rivers in flood, prairie dry as a bone –
One hundred and fourteen horses, one man alone.

Hills and muskeg, forest and rock,
A test for the best at herdin' stock,
Hard work and trouble taken in stride,
A stout-hearted cowboy on a thousand-mile ride.

A worn-out cowboy all sinew and bone,
A livin' legend, ridin' alone,
Good horses delivered on the Rockies' far side;
One more reason for that old prairie pride.

A Five Dollar Cattle Drive

If cattle ride in liners, it saves on wear and tear,
Beats hell out of trailin' cows t'git from here t'there.
Not harpin' on the subject, but it seems not long ago
When our ways by present standards would be judged a mite too slow.

Like when old Mike moved his cows in the spring of forty-five,
Bein' lured by extra cash I was hired for the drive.
It took a half day's ridin' just t'git me there,
Done of course on my time; we agreed that this was fair.

The herd was corralled near midnight by a pale moon's feeble light,
Cows and calves all bawling, shadows driftin' through the night.

Bedded down on the prairie where cold wind fingers probe,
Old Mike snored there beside me, wrapped up in a horsehide robe.
Sleep for me was intermittent, a kid sure feels the cold.
I hoped to grow a thicker skin if I lived t'be that old.

Mike rolled out t'light the fire. Breakfast was at four.
Sidemeat, bannock, and coffee black thawed out my frozen core.
"When a draft disturbs his sleep," he bantered, "a smart man shuts the door."
"Fresh air," says I, "don't bother me, 'twas y'r all-night honkin' snore!"

We lined them out at daybreak, and pointed them up the trail.
Hoof, horn, and curly hide in a crawling serpent's tail.
The sun came up like fire soon warming humpy backs.
At day's end its lingerin' flames flanked our dusty tracks.

It was after sunset when we turned them on the lease.
Six more miles under distant stars, and then I'd sleep in peace.
A long day for short pay in the spring of forty-five,
Earnin' my keep the easy way on a five dollar cattle drive.

Being bound by tradition, this is hard t'say,
But I truly admire the technology that helps us all today.
Cattle ridin' liners, sure as I'm still alive,
Beats hell out of trailin' cows on old Mike's one-day drive.

Still I sometimes wonder, and I'll leave this up to you;
Who in the end is better off, when the day is through?
Old Mike had five dollars and he could spare the time.
Now, can we afford a liner when the banker owns the dime?

W.J. "ROBBIE" ROBERTSON

A retired RCMP staff sergeant (after 40 years' service), Robbie Robertson specializes in poems about the Red-coat Riders of the Plains. An exception is his "Cowboy Poetry", which humorously explains the origins of his literary craft. As a member of the RCMP Veterans Association, Robbie enjoys nothing more than reciting poems in his 1896 NWMP period uniform. He has also appeared on CBC and CTV. Robbie has performed all over the world, ranging far from his High River, Alberta home.

Cowboy Poetry

It goes right back to the days of yore,
A hundred years ago or more.

Cowboys sittin' round a fire
When Hank says, "Bill, I know you're a liar,

"But tell me that tale 'bout the wild cayuse
You rode with one hand while stuffin' snoose.

"Plumb under your lip with the other hand
As he bucked so hard, he shook off his brand.

"But you rode him till he came to a dead stand still.
Won't you tell me that story again, please Bill?"

But Tom said, "Bill, I'm gonna yell
If once more I hear that yarn you tell.

"I'll get so mad, I'll go back home,
Why don't you put it into a po'm?"

And so Bill did before next morn'
And that's how cowboy poetry was born.

FRANK GLEESON

Frank Gleeson is a cattleman and poet who operates the Lone Birch Ranch at Williams Lake, B.C. (with his wife Betty). He has appeared at many poetry festivals across Canada and the U.S., including the big gathering at Elko. "Old Cow" is a fine eulogy from the cowpuncher's stock-in-trade: loyalty to his animals.

Old Cow

I went down to the stockyards, early last spring
I was just gonna visit, not buy me a thing
When this heifer come into the ring, and she looked pretty nice
She's got twin calves and going for the right price
So I took her home and all went pretty well
She was feedin them both there in the corral
But when I turned her out things started to change
She chased one little calf all over the range
She'd knock it, she'd bunt it, she'd kick it away
He's just a young guy and can't live on hay
So I said little fella I'll just take you home
And feed you on pablum till you're fully grown
So I put him in the corral and I thought that's too bad
Cause that little guy he looked pretty sad

I had this old cow that hangs round the yard
She's got one bad leg so getting round's kinda hard
But she gives enough milk for a calf maybe two
And that's more than them fancy young heifers'll do
So I put her in with that little guy
I had nothing to lose, I'll just give it a try
On the first day she ignored him and pushed him away
And then carried on just a munchin her hay
But on her third day there what did I find
That little orphan calf drinkin there from behind
I think what she's sayin and it is just a hunch
If I got extra milk you can stop in for lunch
Now he's just a buckin and tearin around

And happy about this new Mom that he found
And she'd taken to him just like one of her own
It looked like she'd keep him till he's fully grown

It all started at a sale about four years ago
The cows goin cheap and the biddin was slow
When this old cow came into the ring
A quaint looking cow, a gentle old thing
She had a broken off horn and a ratty old tail
Old Tom brought her down from a Central Butte sale
Now old Diff and Sonny were standin up there
A scratchin their heads and pullin their hair
They just can't believe what's happenin out there
The buyers are drunk and they must be asleep
Cause the old cows are goin just less than the sheep
Now old Diff's working hard tryin to get every buck
But on this old cow he's ain't havin much luck
He's hollerin he's chantin he's raisin his voice
But this old cow it's just not their choice
So he turned to me: "Claire give me a bid,
Cause this old cow I just gotta get rid."
I give him a nod and Diff cries out "Sold!"
I felt kinda guilty cause I knew that I stoled
So I took her home and fed her some grain
And every day I could just see her gain
And by the next fall I thought, God ain't that luck
She had the best looking calf on the truck

Now I never knew that day that I bid
She'd take care of that orphan the way that she did
So I hope when the time comes and God calls her up
He will treat her as good as she did that pup
I hope when the time the angels do call
They'll place her alone in her own wooden stall
They'll bed her all down in soft straw and hay
She deserves every bit, she earned all her pay
Now, when my old back aches at night I can't sleep very well

I get out of bed and go down to the corral
I stand by the fence and look up to the sky
I wonder what she's doin as the clouds passin by
Is she eatin is she drinkin is she sleepin alright
Does that bad leg she got keep her up thru the night?

I lean on the fence and just say a prayer
Cause I want her to know that I really care
How she's doin up there beyond the great divide
Is that little orphan calf stickin close by her side
I look up once more and close the corral gate
I gotta get back to bed cause it's getting late
I say my final farewell and I'm feelin real sad
Won't you please take care of her God
She was the best old cow that I ever had.

ROSE BIBBY

*Rose Bibby performs at many gatherings with husband Garth, travelling from their home at Westlock, Alberta. She is the author of several booklets including **Rosebriar Ranch Ramblings** and **Rosie's Rhyme and Reason.** She and Garth have also produced an audio tape, **Hayshakers "Live" at the Bluff.** "Spring Thaw" appeared in **Bards in the Saddle,** a 1997 collection published by the Alberta Cowboy Poetry Association.*

Spring Thaw

I went out to check the calvey cows
in my nightgown, about three.
I weren't expectin' trouble
and they weren't expectin' me!

So when they saw that flannel flappin'
'round my boot tops in the breeze,
They scattered hither-thither
wild of eye and not so pleased.

So then I waddled like a duck
with my nightgown tucked up tight,
And tried to catch those critters
in the beam of my flashlight.

This didn't lighten up the scene
and the bossies were incensed.
And some took leavin' serious
right through a barb-wire fence.

I thought I'd better stop 'em
before they left the yard.
To cut a wider circle 'round
I was off and runnin' hard.

My boot toe caught my nighty
as I danced through the barnyard slop.
Tripped me up and threw me down.
I fell face first...kerplop!

I came up drippin' cow dung,
my nightgown hung in tatters.
And now I smelled so much like them,
my nightie didn't matter.

I tied the fence together
then crept back to the house,
And was met upon the doorway
by my laughin' spouse.

He held his stomach, wiped his tears,
and rolled upon the floor.
He said, "I heard the barb-wire screech
and was comin' out the door...

"When I saw you comin' through the yard,
a cold, wet apparition,
Darlin', don't you think you'll scare the cows
goin' out in that condition?"

BOYD TAYLOR

*Boyd Taylor grew up on a family farm in Saskatchewan. After a long career as a teacher, he retired to ride horses and write cowboy poetry, "because it speaks to the real events and people of the West, using a combination of truth, myth, and humour." He now lives in Wolseley, and continues to ride from his Qu'Appelle Valley spread. This poem appears in his collection, **Mavericks, Strays and Western Ways**, 1998.*

Happy Trails and Full Milk Pails

"Get your water upstream from the herd."
  "Go easy on the rye."
"Never trust a mule's back feet."
  "Keep your long johns dry."

Now while crawling up the creek bank
  And feeling a neck that's kind of pinched,
I can add another mountain motto:
  "Keep your saddle tightly cinched."

DORIS BIRCHAM

Doris Bircham has been partnered with the same man, same ranch, same prairie wind forever. Her family life, nursing career, and ranch experience provide all the inspiration for her writing. She has been a performer and organizer at the Maple Creek Cowboy Poetry Gathering since it began 14 years ago, and her poetry has been widely broadcast on CBC Radio. "Teamwork" and "Cross Breeding Redefined" first appeared in her 1995 book **Teamwork.**

Cross-Breeding Redefined

We own this fleet of used-up trucks
    we mostly use for chores:
a mix of beat-up half tons
    and three old four-by-fours

In some the grills are missing,
    some headlights are plumb gone –
just beat-up chrome and gaping holes
    where Halogens once shone.

Tailgates quit closing long ago,
    tin boxes lean and sag;
the feed truck's kinda hip-slung
    and's wearin' saddlebags.

Blue's lost its power steering,
    Old Grey's axles quit,
windshields are cracked and pitted,
    plus all the seats are split.

Some motors use a little oil,
    rear ends are past their prime
and there's a mess of dents and holes
    punched out beneath the grime.

'Twould take a week to talk about
    the junk piled up inside
those cabs get chucked so doggone full
    there's barely room to ride.

On cold days some refuse to start
    until they've had a pull
and one steel box was bust in two
    by feudin' Angus bulls.

We buy u-joints by the dozens;
    one Dodge has been rewired;
some doors we can't get in or out;
    the 3-ton? It expired.

High on a ridge the old green Ford
    was flat out, headin' west
jumped over that first willow,
    on the second came to rest

right by a slough – it hung there,
    its nose down on the ground,
and when we tried to drag it off
    the darn thing nearly drowned.

You've seen those brand new Dodges,
    those Cummins diesel kind,
well, that's the kind of workin' truck
    that Jake's got on his mind.

But if we bought a truck like that,
    think of its first impression.
It's bound to contemplate its fate
    then lapse into depression.

'Twould learn we've been cross-breedin
    and though this may sound absurd,
it would want to keep its distance
    from our cross-bred truckin' herd.

Teamwork

For more than thirty-odd years now
    Jake and I've been hitched as a team,
and we've carved a few well worn trails
    in fields both barren and green.

Jake pulls his load sure and steady
    while I'm sometimes fast, sometimes slow.
And he handles all kinds of weather
    while I balk in mud and deep snow.

But most time we pull together,
    lean into the harness as one.
For when we turn from each other
    sure enough, a trace becomes undone.

Then our load becomes extra heavy
    with each of us fighting the bit,
and it takes a firm tug on the lines
    before either of us will admit

We need to ease back on our haunches,
    pause awhile, then pull up the slack.
for when our load pushes downhill
    there's no stopping, no turning back.

With calm winds and a load that is light
    there's not too much to upset.
The challenge is climbing steep hills
    when our collars are ringed with sweat.

Where trails are narrow and full of holes
    and rocks are hurting our feet,
some encouragement from our driver
    is sometimes all that we need.

Of course we often wear blinders
    that keep us both staring ahead,
but lately as we jog along
    we glance off to the sides instead.

And we're noticing greener pastures,
  horses standing beside the road
and we know the time is approaching
  when we'll no longer pull our load.

We hope we'll end up in a pasture
  with good grass and clear water to drink,
Side by side we'll lean over the fence
  realizing that we're on the brink

of making that last long trip out.
  When or how no one can explain.
We only hope we both get to meet
  the one who's been holding the reins.

SID MARTY

*Born in England, Sid Marty grew up in Medicine Hat, and worked on horseback for many years as a National Park warden in Alberta and B.C. "Dawn. Jinglin Ponies" appeared in his first collection of verse, **Headwaters**, in 1973. His most recent book, **Sky Humour**, was the first publication of "The Rider with Good Hands". He has also published major works of nonfiction about his beloved Rocky Mountains, which he can admire from the window of his home outside Pincher Creek. Sid Marty's music CD **elsewhere** was released in 2002, and includes "Other People's Cattle".*

Dawn. Jinglin Ponies

Get up in faint cold light
take some oats in a feed bag
coffee will be ready when I return
mist rising on the Maligne river

Half mile walk to toy horses
motionless in wet buck brush
A light frost that was dew
feet get wet
to where they stand
White mare, the bell mare
shakes her head rings her bell
that Mac found twelve years ago
in distant mountains

In cold light and blue shadow
valley and mountain
their white blazes shine
While gentle mare takes the bit
untie the hobbles on one side
horses crowding round the feed bag
their warm breath on my neck
ride back to camp, geldings following
their mare, ride bareback in the cold air
The mare's warm body
between my wet, chilled knees

Other People's Cattle

Met the old man on the streets of town
He didn't look to me like he belonged
Bought him a drink that winter night
He told me something of his life

He said my money's getting lonely from lack of company
And my old truck is tired of defying gravity
The kids all call me "Patches," as round this town I go
I blame that on my mother, for teaching me to sew
And I'm all stove up from fifty years
Of days spent in the saddle
I spent the best years of my life
Raisin' other people's cattle

I went down to the wishing well and I threw a penny in
A face I didn't recognize, looked up at me and grinned
But I get dressed up for Leo's bar, I take a weekend chance
I'm too old for the ladies–but I'm not too old to dance!
Though I'm all stove up from fifty years
Of days spent in the saddle
I spent the best years of my life
Raisin' other people's cattle

It must be thirty years ago
Ginny's pony hit that badger hole
I cursed myself, I cursed my god
But Ginny whispered–"it's not your fault"
Our son lives in the city now
And so we've carried on it seems
It's not as lonely as you think
She comes to hold me in my dreams

I'd hate to calculate the miles of barbed wire
I've strung. Beloved stock dogs I've outlived
The ponies I've worn down
And they laugh to see what the sun has done
To this weathered old red neck
Or how the rope that took my thumb
Has left my hands a wreck

But I wouldn't trade my memories
You know the townie makes me shiver
He drinks his whole life from a glass
Well, I've drunk from the river

My ridin' ropin' days are done
(I don't know why I keep that saddle)
We helped to feed this country, boys
Raisin' other people's cattle

The Rider With Good Hands
(in memorium, David Billington)

In the falling snow
in the field below the garden
A man and a horse are arguing
about barrels, empty barrels in the yellow grass

The rider with good hands
tall in his sheepskin coat
his long black hair dusted with snow,
Knows that cavalcades
Of horsemen who have ridden here before
Are riding here again, through him

His hands upon the reins can check
rebellion in a stubborn mouth
and not give pain. He knows
how the best horses run

How to collect imaginary terrors
trembling between his knees
and turn them into dance

He is a student of arts, roughhewn
but true, and this horse (unruly
as the first draft of a story
or a song) must make
one perfect figure eight

Before the patient rider lets it go
back naked to the windy field, to run
its wild gymkhana with the sun
A perfect figure, done cleanly

And though at last it was stamped down
Though it was covered in a moment by the snow

I see the rider, still,
flowing on four dancing feet
over the sheer dazzle
of an endless, white page

His hands talking tough
talking gentle through the lines
His heavy body lifted
by the beauty of his knowledge
into grace

DORIS DALEY

Proclaimed the "queen of cowboy poets" by her peers, Doris Daley has been a featured performer at every major festival in Canada and the U.S. In 2004 she was named Best Female Cowboy Poet in North America by the Academy of Western Artists. In 2006, she was invited to perform at the 40th annual Folklife Festival in Washington, D.C. by the Smithsonian Institute. She has produced four books of poetry and a CD of her work, **Poetry in Motion.** *Raised in Alberta's ranch country, Doris comes from a gene pool of "ranchers, cowboys, Mounties, good cooks, sorry team ropers, Irish stowaways, bushwhackers, liars, two-steppers and saskatoon pickers." She lives near Calgary with her husband Bob Haysom, a fly-fishing guide on the Bow River. "Bones" and "100 Years from Now" are so cogent and self-explanatory they don't require introductions, but "A Letter to Mr. Russell" may need a brief biography of Charles Russell (1864-1926), the cowboy artist from Montana who almost single-handedly created the iconography of the West: cowboys, natives, and animals. The "Judith" referred to in the poem is the Judith River in Montana.*

Bones

Three cowboys sit on a split rail fence,
Long on bruises, short on sense.
Put 'em together and what do you get –
Besides three pairs of jeans and a pile of debt.

Add 'em all up and the sum of their parts
Is 27 fingers and three broken hearts.
30 pretty toes, only two of them broke,
Hide more scarred than the bark of an oak.

Five good eyes, one made of glass,
Three bum knees and a bad case of gas.
Three strong backs – but all of them achin,
And three mustached smiles filled with Copenhagen.

A bottle of pills for a bad tick-tocker
And a half-full prescription from Dr. Johnny Walker.
A surgeon's nightmare sits on that rail,
But they're married to the range and bonded to the trail.

They'll never be famous, they'll never be wealthy
But they love the life – cause it's so darn healthy.

100 Years From Now

100 years from now, if the world's still in the game,
May the earth recall our footprints, may the wind sing out our names.
May someone turn a page and hearken back upon this time,
May someone sing a cowboy tune and someone spin a rhyme.

History buffs will study us and time will tell its tales
Our lives will be a brittle pile of cold and quaint details.
A scrap of faded photograph, a news headline or two…
But life was so much more, my friend, when the century was new.

100 years from now, don't look back and think me quaint,
Don't judge and call me sinner, don't judge and call me saint.
We lived beneath the arch with a mix of grit and grace,
Just ordinary folk in an extraordinary place.

So 100 years from now hear our ancient voices call,
Know that life was good and the cowboy still rode tall.
Wild flowers filled our valleys and the coyotes were our choir
We knew some wild places that had never known the wire.

We raised stouthearted horses; we'd ride and let 'er rip;
We burned beneath the summer sun and railed at winter's grip.
We took a little courage when the crocus bloomed each spring,
We loved beneath the stars and we heard the night sing.

We buried and we married, we danced and laughed and cried
And there were times we failed, but let the record show we tried.
And sure I have regrets; I made more than one mistake.
If I had it to do over, there are trails I wouldn't take.

But the sun rose up each day; we'd make it through another year,
We'd watch the skies and count our calves and hoist a cup of cheer.
We knew drought and fire and heartache, we knew fat and we knew bone
But we were silver lining people and we never rode alone.

So Friend, if you are reading this 100 years from now
Understand that we were pilgrims who just made it through somehow.
We've crossed the river home and we left but one request:
100 years form now, think back kindly on the west.

And ordinary folk, no special fate, no special claims
But 100 years from now, may the wind sing out your names.
Know the times were good and we rode the best we know.
We loved the west; we kept the faith, 100 years ago.

A Letter to Mr. Russell

Dear Charlie,
Well, I guess they call it progress and progress ain't all bad.
For sure I have advantages that Grandma never had.
But lately I can scarce keep up
With all the lingo in my cup.
It's a chowder I don't want to sup.
  It's sad.

I know it weren't all roses back before they strung the wire.
But each new "improvement" sends us from the fat into the fire.
We'll soldier on, regroup, take stock,
We've still escaped the chopping block.
But Charlie, you should hear us talk.
  A mire.

When the Land belonged to God
No SUVs where bison trod
No ATMs or ATVs
No Enron run by SOBs
No CIA, RCMP
No NAFTA and no GST.

When you waited for a chinook,
No HBO or Selfhelp book
No PCBs or toxic spill
No BLM or Dr. Phil.
No IRS or IRA
No I-15 or Y2K.

When the Judith was plumb hog wild
No Eminem or Destiny's Child
No VCR or DVD
No Bovine Spongeform Encephalopathy
No GPS when cows got loose
No HP Sauce or V8 juice.

Before the whiteman came,
Big Brother didn't run the game.
No CNN on 24/7
No 7-Up or 7-11
No IBM or CD.ROM
No dub dub dub dot west.com

Please send a bronc to breakfast soon
And kick this nonsense to the moon.
Charlie, here's my fervent plea:
When my time is up, may I R.I.P.?
Till then, a prayer for this world and me:
May we get a grip ASAP
     Signed DD

LEE BELLOWS

Lee is a long-time member of the Canadian Professional Cowboys Association. He rode bulls before taking on a career as a rodeo clown and barrel man at events like the Calgary Stampede and Canadian Western Agribition. A lifelong Moose Javian, Lee Bellows now works as a district livestock inspector in Saskatchewan when he isn't performing cowboy poetry at every event within riding distance. "Rodeo Dreams" and "Teresa" have never been published till now. In fact, Lee is a bit skeptical about committing his words to print, and offered me these poems torn from a clipboard.

Rodeo Dreams

Entry fees – road maps
Long miles – cat naps
Arena dust – turnout fines
Warm beer – detour signs
Buzzin flies – morning slack
Flat tire – got no jack
Summer sun – broken barrier
Thrown shoe – find a farrier
Fuel's high – drawin bad
Cops' siren – steaming rad
Bucked off – wounded pride
Phoned home – dog died
Bad cheque – labour list
Skull cramps – swollen wrist
Bad breath – skinned knuckles
But here I am – still chasin buckles

Teresa

My mother said, "Wear clean shorts and never talk to strangers."
She pretty much prepared me for a life that's full of dangers.

But how could she have known about the problems that I'm facin'?
You see, the woman that I'm livin' with has took up barrel racin'.

I didn't see it coming; she was helping leg up my old heelin' horse
Next thing I know they're roarin' round that three-barrelled course.

I'm doin all the cooking while she's in the practice arena;
The kids say my supper tastes like something from Purina.

She's started dressing Fancy, from her belt down to her toes.
Every time they crack the gate, it's a blinkin' fashion show.

We don't go to dances any more, we gotta get right back.
She's workin' two tomorrow and the first one's in the slack.

I do get to help out with the occasional entry fee;
But 'tween the gas and tires, our Visa card needs plastic surgery.

You know this deal all pays off when she makes a decent run.
I sure like to see her smile – Dam', she's having fun!

NEIL MEILI

*Neil Meili was born in Gravelbourg, Saskatchewan, and raised on a ranch along the north shore of Old Wives Lake. His first book of verse, **Cowboys, Poets, and Pilots**, was published in 1995 by New Texas Press, Austin, Texas, where he was also a director of the Austin International Poetry Festival. He has lived a whirlwind of poetic activity ever since, publishing 16 books of poetry, and taking part in poetry strolls and gatherings across the continent. "The Old Dry Guy and the Bath" was taken from **Cowboys, Poets, and Pilots**.*

The Old Dry Guy and the Bath

The old timers were all settin' around the general store
They'd been there forever, and a few days more
Hocking up gossip and spit, an occasional snore

And as it's always been in the West or the East
The one who knew the most said the least
He had a face like old harness and one bad eye
To myself I called him "the old dry guy"

It was real late in the year and the boys were abuzz
Old Jeb had got scalded and burned off some fuzz
He'd been bathing in his kitchen in the old tin tub
And reaching for the kettle to warm up the rub,
Slipping he'd spilt it and lost skin and hair
And the boys were speculatin' how much and where

They'd talked it around three hours or more
When the 'old dry guy' moved his chair by the door
They all got real quiet and leaned close to hear:
"Serves the damn fool right, bathin' this time of year!"

KEN MITCHELL

*Ken Mitchell is a story-teller, playwright and poet, born and raised near Moose Jaw. As an actor, he has performed his work around the globe, and in 1999 was inducted into the Order of Canada for his efforts in "promoting Canadian literature at home and abroad." In 2006 he was invited to the Cucalambe Festival of Country Music and Poetry in Las Tunas, Cuba. "Spook" was originally published in **The Saskatchewan Stockgrower** as a tribute to the 100-year-old cowboy Bill Gomersall; "On the Missouri Coteau" was his first cowboy poem, celebrating the hill country of his heritage.*

Spook

Bill wrangled in the early years, bustin broncos every fall.
a legend from the Cactus Hills, the wrangler Gomersall.
He wasn't much for a rhinestone shirt or slicked-up leather chaps,
packed a sheepskin coat, a 303, an old Ukrainian hat.

But through the southland he's still known for his savvy with a horse
so let him tell the tale of Spook – a cowboy's tale, of course.
"He weren't the fastest steed I had, and he came to me by fluke
but I rode together thirteen years with the gelding I called Spook.

"When I first set eyes on the big white colt, and his outlaw pedigree
I was breakin greens for English Sid, in a corral at Galilee.
Harrisons had sold their herd when the bank called up their lease
and Sid put in a lowball bid on their herd of sorry beasts.

"The White Colt was a renegade, who'd busted all their fences.
They gelded him to calm him down, but that just inflamed his senses.
Never broke him, couldn't sell him; oh he was a fearsome sight,
breakin up the poplar poles, splinters flying left and right.

"My monthly pay at English Sid's was one horse, in trade for sweat,
which cut Sid's cost, and built my herd, and kept me out of debt.
I dreamed then of a high range spread along the Cactus Hills
where a thousand horses could run free, and a man could live fulfilled.

"Sid said, 'He's yohs if you break him.' I started in next day,
a rope hackamore in a pole corral. I gave him lots of space.
Within a month, mebbe less, I could lunge him either side.
I worked without a rein or bit, and never trashed his pride.

"He learned to heel like a shepherd dog; I spoke in nonsense rhyme
and trained him to lead at a gentle touch, though it took a bit of time.
By snowfall he was saddle broke, though snuffy on the bit,
and then one day Len Swanson came, a hunter and a wit.

"Len offered fifty and his good bay mare; he was heading for the buttes,
and needed a big horse built for snow, invisible to coyotes.
Three days later Len was back, blazing eyes and back all hunched,
the colt had spooked and throwed him at the creek by Willowbunch.

"Len sez, 'I chased him two whole days, and lost him at Wood Mountain.
But he run off with my King Rope saddle – so I'm doing long accountin.
Keep the mare and the fifty bucks, just track that bastard down
and shoot him if you have to, but bring that saddle home.'

"I tracked him past the wolvers' caves in the creeks along Big Muddy
Badlands till I found him, his white coat raw and bloody,
up a coulee on Montana side, with a howling coyote pack
circling in the hills above, waiting to attack.

"His bridle was gone. He'd rolled to scrape the saddle off his back
The cinch had twisted round his chest, and was cuttin like an axe.
He staggered to rise, fell in the dust, fought to his feet again.
Watching in the moonlight, I could feel each stab of pain.

"I started in with the songs of old, and kept it up till dawn
till I could edge in close enough to slide a halter on.
Some cowboy poems, and outlaw tales, and calming bits of rhyme.
And I talked to the colt of lessons learned and the trust that comes with time.

"By dawn I'd cut the saddle off, and applied my Rawleigh's salve,
And as he trembled below my knife – for that was all I had –
my blade sliced through the tatters of putrefying flesh
that hung from his neck and withers, a most ungodly mess.

"I trailed him home the hundred miles across the high plateau
and when we reached the pens at Galilee, I turned him in alone.
Swanson got his bay mare back, and his fifty bucks to boot.
And I swore I'd never sell that horse, and I re-named him 'Spook'.

"I didn't ride him for over a year, to ease the torment from his mind.
Then we trained all over again, till we left even words behind.
And we worked together eight long years to buy the Running D ranch,
Rodeo wrangling in the summers, hunting coyote pelts for cash.

"All winter we ranged the Frenchman bluffs, and crossed the Cypress Hills,
the badlands round Big Muddy Lake, Montana's Quadranchie rills.
Spook was like my other half, and I never had no choice,
because he worked for Gomersall, and listened to one voice.

"The ranchers knew me after while; they'd see us riding in,
a fresh-shot partridge in my bag, a stack of coyote skins.
We'd stay up till our eyes bled, drinking schnaps and brew,
shooting bull and cowboy tales, and warbling tunes we knew.

"One March along Wood River, a blizzard began to blow.
The cutbanks 'long its coulees were soon drifted deep in snow,
Left home that morning, lightly dressed, the sky was bright with sun.
but by two o'clock, the blackened sky told of a rising storm.

"The town of Woodrow lay ahead somewhere in that gloom.
I urged Spook to pick up speed, for it had the look of doom.
But the snow grew ever deeper as he plunged and fought.
I had to dismount and lead on foot before his lungs were shot.

"Across the valley through the haze, I spied the distant light
of a coal oil lamp in a lonely shack, flickering in the night.
But the coulee banks were filled with drift, impossible to cross,
and the farm house lamp a mocking sign of our impending loss.

"We pushed along the valley ridge, fighting for each step,
praying for a miracle that might offer some escape,
when we stumbled on a railway line which curved toward the place
where a trestle spanned the dark abyss, and vanished into space.

"The structure shook like a yearling stray, trembling in the wind
I dragged Spook to the trestle edge, where all my hope was pinned.
One step on, his hoof plunged through; he stumbled back in fear
and fought me off like a soul possessed, and then refused to hear.

"He stamped and whimpered like a child, as though he'd lost his trust.
And we staggered back to the coulee bank to find shelter from the blast
I couldn't leave him, but to live – it meant I had to go.
Hunkered there we thought dark thoughts, of freezing in the snow.

"He wouldn't quit, I have to admit, not that big white horse.
He started pushing with his head, like a trainer plying force.
We approached again the wooden bridge and took another look.
I brushed snow from the first two ties to show how they were put.

"Then I took my box of matches out and lit a bunch at once,
a flare so he could see his footing, and I gave his hoof a nudge.
And then by god, he got it, and he took a couple more
And followed me 'cross the swaying bridge, as I cleared the ties before.

"In a while we reached the shack with the burning coal oil lamp
and a startled family took us in, though I looked like a frozen tramp.
Spook and I spent that night in their straw-filled dugout shed
and I sank to my knees and thanked the Lord for a horse that used its head.

"He weren't the fastest mount I had, and he came to be me by fluke
But I rode together thirteen years with the outlaw I called Spook."
Thus spoke the man who roamed the land on horseback every fall,
The cowboy of the Cactus Hills, the legend Gomersall.

On The Missouri Coteau

Sure good to see ole Henk again ridin with our crew
along the trail on the big coteau. Bin years since he was through.
He left here for the rodeo, then took up tendin bar
and livin the life of a vagabond with a banjo and guitar.

But there's heavy lines across his face and his eyes seem kinda dull
as if them years he spent down South been etched inside his skull.
"Boys," sez he, "I'm tickled green to be sitting by your fire
cause all the fancy bars I've seen can't set a tone no higher.

"Way out here on the high plateau your spirit gets a shake
like the smell of coffee on the boil, a thing you don't mistake.
That grub we ate was what I craved, each night in every town.
Your venison and biscuit pie in taverns can't be found.

"Oh, I've sampled horses' doovers in the bistros of Orleans
and all the bins on the Broadway – but they can't match Donny's beans.
And smart talk? Well, I heard lots, in some courtrooms here and there
but I tell you men, my learning began when I heared ol' Wally swear.

"As for music, I took in a few big concerts in my days,
but I still prefer the steady purr of a crackling pinewood blaze.
Or the plaintive howl of a coyote prowling through yon aspen wood
is gonna affect the hair on your neck, like no soprano could.

"'I've wandered the world, looked at great art, your Leonardos and Vince Van Go,
but if you wanta study a masterpiece, take a sunset on the coteau.
Look at it there, all purple and gold, 'gainst a blue like a robin's egg.
No painter I know can capture the flow of those shapes on heaven's lake.

"So pour me out another cup of Slim's black-as-hades brew;
the coffees I been sippin late are thin as Moose Jaw stew.
I'll just sit and reflect a bit on the loneliness of bars,
and the music of the Big Coteau, and the distances of stars."

THELMA POIRER

*Thelma Poirier is a member of the Anderson clan of Fir Mountain, a horse-ranching dynasty that goes back to pioneer days. After a lifetime raising cattle with her husband Emile in the rangeland around Wood Mountain, Saskatchewan she has moved to the town of Glentworth, where she continues to write poetry. "Line Rider" is from a 1992 collection, **Grasslands**. Thelma represented Canada at the Elko gathering in 1992, and has returned many times since.*

Line Rider

from Eastend to the Big Muddy
I was hired to throw back strays
horses, perhaps with glanders
throw them back across the line
the line, two strands of barbed wire
stretched between two countries

those were rough-out days –
when I left the Post
the horses I rode were broncs
remounts when I returned
the Mounties knew how to get the most
out of the man

slow days I took the squeaks
out of my saddle
nights I hit the cow camps
card games in Montana

summer passed
easy in the saddle

ANDREW SUKNASKI

A leading poet of the Western Canada literary renaissance, Andy Suknaski was born on his family homestead near Wood Mountain, Saskatchewan in 1942. In a long and productive literary career, he first began publishing his own work at Elfin Press. In 1976, Macmillan published **Wood Mountain Poems,** *edited by Al Purdy, and international acclaim followed, along with many more books of verse.* **Wood Mountain Poems** *has recently been reprinted by Hagios Press. "Western Prayer" is the final poem in that collection.*

Western Prayer

time poet
to put aside what you came to
leaving all else
behind

time to unsaddle
this lame horse ridden into ancestral dust
and cease living like an Indian
of old

time to do things with the hands
working all seasons
with pride
and three weeks vacation
each year

time to tie this dream horse to a star
and walk
ordinary earth

MARK ELFORD

McCord, Saskatchewan rancher Mark Elford is also a musical performer. "The Great Divide" was written as a tribute to his father who died shortly after Mark's brother Wes was killed hauling hay. Mark set the poem to music and recorded it for an audio cassette **The Great Divide,** *performed by a country-gospel band, Family Reunion.*

The Great Divide

He raised us up high up on the great divide
We raised white face cattle, rode stocking ponies
Out along the north side
Wearin' high-heeled boots and wide-brimmed hat
You could see the world like that
Livin' out along the great divide.

Big strong man with calloused hands
Taught us how to work the land
And to put out hard
From sun to sun.
Supper over, and time for bed
Mom made sure the Bible got read, they were a real team
And growin' up was fun.

You learned it young and I did too
Bein' a cowboy ain't hard to do, it's in the way you think
Not the clothes you wear.
Together then we rode the range,
Thought that things would never change, makin a livin
And doin' our share.

It was way up there where it's wild and free
The water chooses sea from sea, that's where you went ahead
Left him and me.
The cows still run out on the top
That part won't ever stop, but the great divide
Has new meaning for me.

He raised us high up on the great divide...
We raised white faced cattle, rode stocking ponies
Out along the north side.
Wearin' high-heeled boots and a wide-brimmed hat
You could see the world like that
Livin' out along the great divide.

JUDY HOPKINS

Judy Hopkins was raised on a farm near Melfort, Saskatchewan. She is much intrigued by the "spirituality of horses" and recently performed at the Royal Saskatchewan Museum's Cowboy Poetry Festival in Regina. Her self-published book **Fed From Different Streams** *appeared in 2000. It included "Wonder Dog", a sly testimony to the poetic naming of animals. As for her age . . . .*

Wonder Dog

My friend's little dog
was black and white
and the way she moved cattle
was his heart's delight.

She'd stuff 'em through the gates
and push 'em through the chutes
and master any beast
mounted on four hooves.

Folks would flock
from miles around
to see that little pooch,
belly slinkin to the ground.

Some folks who were visitin',
Drawn by the dog's fame,
Were impressed and asked,
"What's the little dog's name?"

My friend stood with a grin
That stretched from ear to ear
And laughingly choked out,
"The dog's name is Brassiere

because she provides some support
and lots of protection.
She heads 'em up and points 'em
In the right direction!"

DAVE PRATT

Dave Pratt is a Cree-Dakota of the Gordon First Nation in Saskatchewan, and has worked across Canada and the U.S. as a rodeo rider and cowboy. He was a performer at Elko in 1996, and Calgary's Cowboy Festival in 1997. His first book, **A Cowboy Rides Away,** *was published in 1997. The title poem is dedicated to his friend Lionel Poitras, a Cree-born RCMP officer who died while taking part in a rodeo at Yorkton.*

A Cowboy Rides Away
(Tribute to a fallen partner and friend, Lionel Poitras)

A cowboy made his last run
When he drew his final steer,
He was up in the doggin, at Yorkton
The last rodeo of the year.

It won't be the same without him,
But we know he'll be okay
Our hats are off, to a fallen partner
As a cowboy rides away.

And will God pay attention
To the cowboy mounted there,
When he rides to the gates of Heaven
Trophy buckle gleaming, his life to share?

Lord, please don't flag him out,
Don't delay him at the gate.
This cowboy's already earned his dues,
And his entry fees are paid.

All he needs is one fast horse
And a steer that runs straight and true,
I know his judge is gonna be fair
And the timer is too.

And God, if you could do his hazin'
That would be better than alright,
It would make us awful grateful,
And we'd get better sleep tonight.

Lord, thanks a lot for listening
To us cowboys down this way,
And welcome him to your arena
As this cowboy rides today.

MIKE PUHALLO

A cattle rancher who now lives near Kamloops, B.C., Mike Puhallo became a rodeo cowboy at the age of 16, and rode the circuit for over twenty years. He has published three volumes of cowboy verse: **Rhymes on the Range, Still Rhymin' on the Range,** *and* **Can't Stop Rhymin' on the Range.** *"The Man in the Moon" appeared in the first book, published by Hancock House. It is on his first CD,* **The Smell of Sage and Pine.**

The Man in the Moon

I laid on my back in the cool, damp grass,
about an hour or more,
Just beyond the light of the coal-oil lamp
that shone through the bunkhouse door.

Old Drake came by,
nearly tripped on me and asked,
"Mikey, what are you doin'?"
I said, "Hush up, Jack, and sit a spell.
I'm waitin' for the man in the moon!"

You see, I had my radio there
an' history was in the makin'.
There were things goin' on in the clear night sky
that would set your head to shakin'.

A few at a time, the rest of the crew
came out to join us there,
Till ten cowboys lay in the cool, damp grass
and stared up through the clear night air.

Now that old transistor crackled with static,
At times it was damned hard to hear.
But the rising moon was so big and bright
I'd never seen it so near.

Now them folks on the radio chattered on so
about this lunar landing,
an' most of it was technical junk
Beyond my understanding.

Then we heard that spaceman say something
about one small step for man.
We all hung in close to the radio
to listen the best we can.

Now a lotta that broadcast was lost to us
Between the static and the coyotes' tune.
But we caught enough to know darn well
A man was on the moon.

Now a cowboy can't stay up that late,
the morning comes too soon.
So we drank to his health and each in turn
said "Good night" to the man in the moon.

But it must have been late when I found my bunk,
I slept till nearly four.
And it was my turn to jingle the horses
and knock at the old cook's door.

By the time I had the jingle done
and ran those ponies in,
Dawn was breakin' in the eastern sky
and the moon was pale and thin.

No time to think of spacemen now,
just grab some breakfast and leave on a trot.
There's a gather to make and cows to move
before the sun gets hot.

A lot of summers have come and gone
since that one at Douglas Lake.
But none that did so much to mold
the kind of man I'd make.

It was a season full of adventure,
there's lots of memories there.
Like when Darwin's horse pitched him in the creek,
Or the time Red roped a bear.

But by far my fondest memory
of a summer that ended too soon
Was ten cowboys sprawled in the cool, damp grass
Jes' watchin' the man in the moon.

ANNE SLADE

*Ann Slade lives with her husband Robert on their ranch in the Cypress Hills of Saskatchewan. She is the author of **Denim, Felt and Leather**, as well as a book and tape she co-authored with her friend Doris Bircham, **Pastures, Ponies and Pals**. In their latest project, the two worked with Thelma Poirier to create a book called **A Voice of Her Own**, published in 2006 by University of Calgary Press. All three poems included here appeared in Bards in the Saddle, a collection of the Alberta Cowboy Poetry Association, published in 1997 by Hancock House.*

Cowboy Wake

"Now lass," he said, from his hospital bed,
"You'll do what I ask, I can tell.
Before I'm laid to rest, take a case of the best
to my room at the Cactus Hotel.

"There's no fences to mend with my old friends
though no doubt they've a thirst to slake.
Wipe those tears from your eyes, kiss this old man good-bye
and look after those plans for my wake."

Then just before dawn, they told her he'd gone
and she wasted no time with tears.
She called up the hands who'd helped rope and brand
with her grandfather over the years.

The word travelled far, that they'd set up a bar
in his room at the Cactus Hotel.
His pals drifted in and joined with his kin
to bid the old wrangler farewell.

Recallin' the past, they'd raise up a glass
to their friend laid out by the bed.
Then singin' his praise, they'd toast the old days
recountin' the wise words he'd said.

How in his rough way, he'd taken each day
as a gift to enjoy and share.
And though he was gone, they each carried on
as if the old man was still there.

They'd talk man to man and pat the cold hand
of their pardner laid out with pride.
Sing cowpunchin' songs, to help him along
on his trek cross the Great Divide.

And so for his sake, cowhands at the wake
heeded the things he had asked.
For three days and nights, some sober, some tight,
they reminisced right to the last.

They carried him down, to the main street in town
mounted horse, and riding abreast
of the horse-drawn hearse, to the small country church
where they laid our old friend to rest.

Barb-Wire Vault

When we had been wed, just a short time, he said,
"Now Honey, here's a good job for you.
While I'm away, check those heifers each day,
there's one of them overdue."

I beamed with pride, though nervous inside
this city gal could finally show
that she could fit in, so keen to begin,
I waved as I watched him go.

That very first day, I went out right away,
checking heifers who weren't even cross.
Why they didn't mind when I viewed their behinds
and I figured that I was the boss.

But I wasn't, I'm confessin', I learned my lesson
and honestly, this is no yarn,
one heifer was complainin', she seemed to be strainin',
so I chased her towards the barn.

She didn't want to go, but how could I know
her water broke when she stood up.
She sniffed the air, like she smelled calf somewhere,
and here's where I ran out of luck.

She turned around, kinda pawin' the ground,
and I didn't think it my place
to stay where I was, so I took off because
I didn't like the look on her face.

I raced for the fence, which didn't make much sense
'cause heifers run faster than me.
I shoulda jumped higher, but I hit the top wire,
Caught my jeans just above the knee.

So I'm hangin' down with my hand on the ground
and her snotty nose in my face.
Cow shit in my hair and my boots in the air,
oh gawd, what an awful disgrace!

She huffed and snorted and kinda cavorted,
like she was playin' with me.
She'd back up and stare but she was right there
when I'd reach for that barb in my knee.

Her tail was a mess and I woulda cared less,
'cept she used it to ward off the flies.
And the pieces of crud, mixed in with wet mud
speckled my nose and my eyes.

I hung from the wire, until she got tired
and moved off towards the trees,
then I disconnected before she objected,
thankful to finally be freed.

When I got in that night, I thought over my plight
and I knew that I was at fault.
My green misreadin's what sent her stampedin'
and taught me the barb-wire vault.

Cowboy Blessing

May the rains fall on your pastures
and the grass grow belly high.
May your calves get fat and sassy
and none of your cows be dry.
May your horse be sure-footed
and blessed with good cow sense.
May your neighbours lend a hand
when it's time to mend the fence.
May the sun shine on your crops
when you harvest in the fall.
May your handshake be considered
your word by one and all.
When your life is filled with happiness
or when it's sad and gray,
May those you love be with you
to share each blessed day.

BRYN THIESSEN

Bryn is a veteran performer who lives with his family on the Helmer Creek Ranch near Sundre, Alberta. He is also a popular preacher. His distinctive handlebar moustache – sixteen inches from tip to tip – has become a much-admired feature at every cowboy poetry event in the west. "The Prairie Breeze" was published in his illustrated collection **Wind in the Pines** *(Spur Graphics, Sundre, 1994). "Victorian Verse" appeared in* **Bards in the Saddle** *(Hancock House, 1997).*

The Prairie Breeze

Look! There's another –
Third one this week!
Some paper talking about
That ozone layer leak.
Now that isn't new,
Naw, it's been around a while,
But when I see the reason
It kind of makes me smile.

It seems that some scientists –
Including Suzuki –
Well they don't blame radiation,
Or microwaves gone kooky.
No, they say
The reason for that hole,
Well it comes from cattle
And the air that they blow.

Now any of us
Who raise the bovine breed,
Know they have certain –
Functional needs.
And if it's time
That they find that relief,
The resulting occurrence
Is seldom pleasant or brief.

Now I'll agree
There are those who know more
Than one who left early
Educational doors,
But even Lee Pitts
And that poet named Baxter
Have pondered this question
While riding through pastures.

And I think they'd agree
With my fervent wish,
That the problem was Tofu,
Chicken or fish.
"But no," say the experts,
"They cause us no grief.
When we look for a problem,
We seem to find beef."

"It's when cows digest,"
Or so the article explains,
"When they break down their vegetation
It produces methane.
This is then passed
Through intestinal tracts,
Till it's expelled with some force
Out the back."

Now with this I'll agree,
But what I find hard to swallow
Is that methane's the reason
That ozone goes hollow.
But if it's true,
Well I'll take my chances
That the ozone will last
While the northern light dances.

Because I'm far more worried
Of what we've done to the land
By the things that we've built
With our heart and our hands.
So I'll just keep riding,
A good horse between my knees,
And not be too worried
About a little
   "Prairie Breeze".

Victorian Verse

Through yonder portal shines the light;
Dawn breaking—where's gone the night?
I rise from canvas bed,
Run my nose and scratch my head,
And listen to the eerie sounds
Of bodies rising from the ground.

O pray tell, what manner of men are these
Whose legs are bowed in parentheses?
I've come back on another time it seems;
'Tis like a bad midsummer night's dream.
So I struggle to break free.
O what fools these mortal men can be!

Then the sun rises past the hill,
And in the wind I feel a chill.
Then I awake in clammy sweat.
'Twas but a dream, yet I can't forget!
And so I take my quill in hand
To write the words I understand.

But this dream could mean my death;
For once these hands, they wrote *Macbeth*.
But now it seems they go untrue,
For I just wrote *Taming a Horse to Show*.
And my greatest love story written yet
Comes out as *Roany and a Lariat*!

So I fear that I must change my name
Lest folks should hear, think me insane.
I'll call myself Billy Rattling Lance.
And in my future should I have the chance,
I'll leave this earth as I know it
And come back down as a cowboy poet!

PHYLLIS RATHWELL

Hatched on a hot rock between the Cypress Hills and the Great Sand Hills, Phyllis raises Angus cattle near Rockglen, Saskatchewan. Refusing to give in to BSE, drought, grasshoppers, cranky men, or common sense, she loves the ranching way of life. She claims to be "equally (in)competent at workin' cattle, checkin' pens, fencin', balin', cussin' gates an' ridin' the grub line." In order to finance these habits, she is also the principal of Rockglen School. "While You're Up" and "Pat's Advice" both offer her characteristically dry comment on domestic politics. Phyllis has been a featured performer at gatherings from Durango, Colorado to Stony Plain, Alberta. Her publications include two books, **Friends and Neighbours, Tried and True** *and* **Range, Riders and Rhymes** *as well as a tape with Terri Mason and Doris Daley,* **Three Babes On A Bale.**

While You're Up

Four little words I'm sick of, that make me roll my eyes
Aren't foul or all four lettered, but they sure antagonize

I'd like to start a campaign to eliminate that phrase
"Honey, while you're up" – It 's making me half crazed

"Honey, while you're up could ya just turn up the heat?
And while you're doin' that, can ya fix something to eat?"

"While you're up I'd like a coffee," "Can ya find the new phone book?"
"I think I heard a car pull in, while you're up just take a look."

It isn't just inside the house, it can happen anywhere!
If I turn and look toward the barn, it's "Honey, while you're there

Can you fetch me my new lariat? An' I'll need the calving chains,
Some boluses an' 'lectrolytes"…it gives me a real pain.

In harvest if I'm haulin' wheat, it's "While you dump this load…
Could you make me lunch and check the bulls… there's one out on the road."

In the middle of the night, too… I can't escape no how
It's, "Honey while you're up, could you run out an' check the cows?"

"While you're up just switch the channel" "While you're up there grab my hat"
"While you're there I need a pencil, and adjust the thermostat."

Oh, I don't see any end to this. When the pearly gates I see
I'll likely hear his far-off voice, "While you're up there, pray for me."

Pat's Advice

It was a normal enough year,
(we were a month or so behind)
Needed an extra pair o' hands
an' wanted the useful kind.

Pat said he had some advice
and for sure, it was all free
"Don't hire a kid from an Angus place,"
was what Pat said to me.

Now, I was a mite surprised,
'cause Pat, he's an Angus man.
He winked as he 'splained how
he'd arrived at his hiring plan.

"The kid from an Angus place," he said,
"can't do what he don't know how.
He's never had to pull a calf
or range-treat an Angus cow.

"He's never trimmed a curled-up toe
or treated a pendulous bag.
He don't know how to dehorn a steer
an' a prolapse'd make him gag.

"He's never helped a calf mother-up
or seen a sunburned udder,
Nor searched the range for a baby
Abandoned by its mother.

"The Angus-ranch kid, he's lazy
his horse is downright fat.
He's great at yarnin' an' singin'
But you don't want to pay for that.

"If you really want a bargain
get a kid from a Hereford place
He can do the vettin' you need done
he'll be thin, won't take up much space.

"He'll be lean an' mean an' rangy
an' he'll be grateful to ya, honey
'Cause he ain't used to reg'lar meals,
an' he sure ain't used to money!"

POET'S NOTE: Pat Fitzpatrick was a rancher in the Wood
Mountain area of Saskatchewan. He told me he had to come
up with an excuse for being at Hereford bull sales – so he'd
explain that he was looking for a hired man… when he
actually was there for the free whiskey… He was a staunch
supporter of rodeo and youth, a great friend, and someone
who was comfortable in his boots. He is missed.

WAYNE "SLIM" MITCHELL

Slim Mitchell grew up on the XM Bar ranch near Moose Jaw, where he now raises a young family, a herd of pot-bellied pigs, a rabbit called Baxter Black, and hope for the future. He began performing as a Stompin' Tom Connors impersonator, took up cowboy poetry, and appeared at many cowboy poetry events, usually with Bill Gomersall and the Mitchell Boys. "Colin's Grove" is located on his Moose Javian acreage.

Colin's Grove

When I walk in Colin's Grove, the memories come back clear.
My Old Man walks beside me; I feel his spirit here.
The wind is whistling as we walk, it's peaceful where we rove.
We stop a spell when we spy the plough that first tilled Colin's Grove.

We talk about the hillside, and how the blow-dirt shaped its line
And how we planned this grove of trees, the aspens and the pines.
He drove the tractor; I rode the plow – like yesterday it seems --
And now I walk and reminisce in this forest of our dreams.

This Scotch pine stands to mark the spot his final plough was cast,
and others have grown to join him in this garden of our past.
We plant each tree to mark the time when loved ones venture on,
And gather round to toast their lives, and sing till light of dawn.

A stone cairn stands along the path, by the entrance to a clearing.
A bench of stone surrounds the wheel off some McCormack-Deering,
The iron scorched a reddish hue (it's seen some better days).
Let's fill it up with firewood and set the pile ablaze.

At the fire you may hear about the sayings of my Dad,
How gatherin' friends and family was a passion that he had.
He worked so hard at teaching us, left big-league boots to fill,
Now I try to share his wisdom in this grove on Colin's Hill.

Come join us at the fire. We'll relive those golden times.
We'll hear old tales of ranching life, chant poetry in rhymes.
You'll meet cowgirls, horses, outlaws, and men that madness drove
Through the roar of life till they found peace, in the trees of Colin's Grove.

SHERI-D WILSON

Calgary poet sheri-d wilson – "The Mama of Dada" – is probably the most radical cowboy poet in Canada. She is a multi-talented spoken word artist – writer, actor and dancer – whose work has electrified audiences everywhere. She has published six books of poetry and released a powerful CD called **sweet taste of lightning.** *"Fortis et Liber" is her celebratory anthem of freedom and femininity, published here for the first time. Several of her video poems were screened on BRAVO! She has won almost every performance poetry contest going, including the title of Heavyweight of Poetry, USA, in a 2003 Bumbershoot Bout against Andrei Codrescu. Her latest book,* **Re:Zoom,** *from Frontenac House, won the 2006 Alberta Book Award for Best Poetry Book. She has recently returned to her Alberta roots, and in 2004 founded the Calgary International Spoken Word Festival, of which she is the Artistic Director. And she wrangles horses.*

Fortis Et Liber

Oh, I love you Alberta
Big sky beautiful you, strong woman, ruff and soft soft blue
I'm sitting right in the middle of miles of you
High on my ponderosa pony
Saddle smooth and sexy beneath me
I want to ride the range of your possibility
I'm Alberta bound baby; hear the silence of your immensity
I want to touch the horizon of your immeasurable light
Ride the westerly wind of your raven flight
Pow
Pow wow
Let's go
Golden trail. Light sinks, just west of highway 22
As me and mini gallop wild-west to the crest of you
Ah! Your light stops us in our horseshoe tracks in awe
Even your shadows fall gold – alchemist maw
In the background your a capella sky that impossible colour
It would seem, beyond, beneath me ponderosa pony ponders –
amber dream
Find a feather
Find a feather

There's something ancient about you,
>   buried deep in your badland bones
Hoodoo voodoo queen,
>   your heavenly body sings aurora high notes - flood lights,
>   I ignite - this night - firefly rare
I am tongue tied, moonified,
>   I am sanctified, satisfied as a studified mare
By your light – Oh Alberta, your light turns me on – Bar Bonbon
My big horse Mini, is of course,
>   all a' whinny, all a shimmy beneath me, over you
Oh yeah,
>   I want to drink of your milky-way river
I want to bucking-bronc scream from your highest peak
Mount Columbia 13,000 feet
Hey lucky stars up there…thanks for birthing me here…
Certified Albertafied – Grade A Canadian girl

I fell for you as a kid
Stubbed my toes on your gopher holes
Shucked the pearl from your prairie oyster, witnessed first-time
eyes of newborn foals, picked whole bouquets of full rushes for
my mother, played hide-n-seek between jails and hails and bales
of hay like none other, like every other, tumbling tumbleweed
Looked into the forbidden eyes of grizzly, bare
Alberta bound baby,
>   stars fall in the mischief of your eyes as we drop off
Like late season flies,
>   or crab-apples wind plucked from their branches
And when we rise, in the morning,
>   ad manum from more
You Chinook arch above the foothill floor,
>   merge and diverge, animal to the core
Through dawn's early dew,
>   we roll against the earth moving earth
Like a couple of crazy coyotes,
>   howling with instinct
Half wrangling, half untangling –
>   sliding across the slippery Prairie grass

Cacophonous, as one,
      in the path of your bright morn-light stream
Cream all buttermilk,
      pussy willows and crocuses as we stream-steam
Black gold. Light crude.
      You've got gas- it's nasty
It's natural.
      It's rude
      It's our earth
      Our drinking water.

Saddle up ponderosa pony
Pow
Pow Wow
Let's go
I turn –
And O no, I smell winter in the air
Let's get home before she snaps her snare
Gotta put the plastic on the windows
Suddenly it's freezing, my skin is peeling off my face
My only prayer is thermal underwear
Get me out of this hideous place
Alberta, you're a brutal hard uncompromising croon
And I hate you and I want to leave you,
      live somewhere else that's warm, I moan
And just when I'm ready to throw in the bone,
      I smell my first lilac of spring breath – buzzing bees swarm
      bring honeycomb
And that's when I know, these Buffalo plains, they're home
Big sky beautiful you
Strong woman in the ruff, oh yeah, of blue
Wild rose tough; you're my heartland shaman guru
You're Gods country, for God's sake
Pow
Pow Wow
You're a Goddess country, for Goddess's sake
Goddess

DENIS NAGEL

Denis Nagel is a veterinarian who works out of Crossfield, Alberta. He was born at Crane Valley, Saskatchewan., where he fell under the tutelage of Leonard Swanson, a rough-and-ready wrangler from the hills. Denis grew up on a farm and worked many years on cattle ranches, where he took up the writing of cowboy poetry. He still trains and rides horses. "The Day Leonard Taught me to Chew Snuff", his first published poem, appeared in Canadian Folk Music Bulletin, Vol. 25, 1991.

The Day Leonard Taught Me to Chew Snuff

I come from hard-grass country where folks don't go a bunch,
Where the ground's dry as pavement and the gophers pack a lunch.
And in that hard-grass country for a boy to be a man
He's got one day to take a dip from a Copenhagen can.
Leonard was a friend of mine though fifty years my senior:
Tough as boiled owl shit, and he didn't smell much cleaner.

We were talkin' of shootin' coyotes at Leonard's camp one day,
But when you're only ten years old you don't get much to say.
Well he reached down into his shirt and pulled his can of snuff,
He tapped the lid and took a chew and said, "Think yer man enough?"
"Yer goddam right I'm man enough, I'll show ya how it's done."
I jammed three fingers way down deep and took a good-sized one.

He showed me how to hold it between my gum and lip
Then looked me right in the eyes and said, "Only sissies spit!"
My mouth was fillin' up as my saliva began to run –
And then I started wonderin' what I had gone and done.
So I summoned up my courage and said, "Let's go to town."
As my courage was comin' up, it met that snuff juice goin' down.

I suddenly felt warmer and my neck began to sweat
And I got a sinkin' feeling that my snuff ain't settled yet.
I don't know how it happened but the room began to spin
And I began to realize the world of hurt I'm in.
Then I began to retchin' just like a sickly pup –
I barfed out bile and breakfast, and then my boots came up.

I thought I'd met my maker, my insides must be drained.
But I didn't get off so easy, and I chucked her up again.
Now that was twenty years ago when I took my first dip.
And to this day I got a pinch between my gum and lip.
I don't know why I do it; you'd think I had enough.
Like you, I often wonder why I chew the goddam stuff.

PHYLLIS WHEATON

*A rising star on the Calgary music scene, Phyllis launched a CD, **The First Song**, from Alchemy Studio in 2006. Born in northern Ontario, she grew up on a farm in Manitoba. With a tender ear and inquiring heart, she has written about cowboys, war vets, farmers and working Canadians. Last fall, she took her guitar to schools in Scotland to teach students the history of the Scottish migration to Canada. "No Ordinary Cowboy" was performed at the 2006 Pincher Creek gathering.*

No Ordinary Cowboy

Cowboy, Cowboy, where'd you ride in from,
A different bar, a different town and you arrive alone.
Cowboy, if the range is where you spend your days,
Where'd you learn to hold and move in that seductive way?

His hair was long and silver, wide-brimmed hat and eyes of coal
Gray moustache and a rugged smile, not young but still not old
He was hungry for the quest, they were hungry for the dance.
No one refused to be embraced by the cowboy's expert hands.

No ordinary cowboy, no ordinary Saturday.
His leather boots will burn the hardwood
His leather soul will leave alone.

From the moment she accepted, he took her in his arms.
She felt like she was the only person in the room
He moved from the youngest to the most experienced hips,
Exhausted every female with his twirling dives and dips.

No ordinary cowboy left the opposition green
He was every man's nemesis and every woman's dream.
Cowboy cowboy, why'd you come in from the range?
Did your lover let you down, are you seeking some revenge?

Are you here to tease the women, or to anger all the men.
Cowboy, why don't you let someone in?

Women tried to tame him, even tried to take him home.
By his toughened resignation, he always left alone.
A final parting gesture, drank a pint in two big sips
Grabbed the nearest barmaid and beer-kissed her on the lips.

No one knew his story, secrets of his heart of stone.
His leather boots had burned the hardwood,
His leather soul had left alone.

CORB LUND

One of the most successful Western bands in the country, Corb Lund and The Hurtin'
Albertans have toured Australia, Europe and the U.S. They won a "Roots and
Traditional Album of the Year" Juno at the 2006 awards in Halifax, and were
featured in Universal Pictures' theatrical release Slither. Despite his spectacular young
career, Corb Lund remains true to his family roots and Taber, Alberta, heritage.
There he rode, herded, and rodeoed for several years before heading for Edmonton,
where he now makes his home. "The Rodeo's Over" can be heard on his latest CD,
Hair in My Eyes Like a Highland Steer. *Other poems/lyrics are to be found on his*
website: www.corblund.com

The Rodeo's Over

The rodeo's over, the folks have gone home
And the cowboys are all down the road
Well boys, she was a good un, we kicked a hole in the sky
And even the rank ones got rode
It was as wild as they come and it was almighty western
And none of us thought it would end
But finish it did, with a bang and a whimper
And now I must leave you my friend

We may do it again in some future season
But somehow it won't be the same
Cuz our draws will be different and our injuries healed
And it's likely the weather will change
So take from the lessons and be glad for the memories
of the days that we rode in the sun
for after today there'll be no man can claim
that we didn't have us a good run

so burn all the blankets and dry all the tears
we can always go further out west
and I'll meet you out there in the vastness somewhere
I swear it but first I must rest.

PERMISSIONS